THREE TIMES A DAY
SIMPLE & STYLISH

BY

MARILOU & ALEXANDRE
CHAMPAGNE

3 times a day

SIMPLE AND STYLISH

AMBROSIA

THREE TIMES A DAY: SIMPLE & STYLISH
MARILOU & ALEXANDRE CHAMPAGNE

––––––––

Creative director & text by: Marilou
Photographer: Alexandre Champagne
**Cover photograph, and photos pages
2, 14, 20, 60, 266, 294, 298, 304, 314, 315 and 320:** Andréanne Gauthier
Art director & graphic design: Anne Sylvestre
Culinary consultant: Véronique Paradis
Assistant food stylist: Andréane Beaudin
Translator: Anna Phelan
Project coordinators: Sofia Oukass and Marie Guarnera
Nutritionist: Catherine Lefebvre

Under the direction of Antoine Ross-Trempe

––––––––

This edition published in English in Canada in 2017 by House of Anansi Press Inc.
128 Sterling Road, Lower Level
Toronto, ON M6R 2B7
Tel. 416-363-4343
Fax 416-363-1017
www.houseofanansi.com

LIBRARY AND ARCHIVES CANADA CATALOGUING IN PUBLICATION

Champagne, Marilou
[Trois fois par jour. English]
Three times a day : simple and stylish / Marilou & Alexandre Champagne.

Includes indexes.
Translation of: Trois fois par jour : deuxième tome.
Issued in print and electronic formats.
ISBN 978-1-4870-0244-2 (hardcover).—ISBN 978-1-4870-0245-9 (EPUB).—
ISBN 978-1-4870-0246-6 (MOBI)

1. Cooking. 2. Cookbooks. I. Champagne, Alexandre, 1985–, photographer
II. Title. III. Title: Trois fois par jour. English.

TX714.C45513 2017   641.5   C2017-901301-7
                                                          C2017-901302-5

*We acknowledge for their financial support of our publishing program
the Canada Council for the Arts, the Ontario Arts Council, and the Government of
Canada through the Canada Book Fund.*

PRINTED AND BOUND IN CANADA

INTRODUCTION

Two years have passed between the release of my first book and this one, and it's been a trying time but also a rewarding one. Reflecting on everything that has happened to me over these last months, I can't help but feel bolstered and empowered by a growing sense of confidence that, little by little, is replacing the feeling of emptiness that overwhelmed me before I wrote *Three Times a Day*.

I feel more calm and more relaxed. I've seen ample proof that something much bigger than me is making sure that whatever happens to me is for the best . . . always. The best that brings smiles, as well as the best that brings tears. I've learned to let sadness and joy coexist and watch them dance together through my life . . . and find it all beautiful. So, I could introduce this book by describing the succulent recipes it contains and say that writing it was nothing but fun. I could assure you that Alex and I are a perfect team and that my relationship with food is the stuff of fairy tales, and so on, and say this book is a dream come true. But I'd be lying.

The truth is, creating this book was one of the most difficult things I've ever done and, at the same time, one of the most wonderful.

Because I learned . . . a lot.

Over the course of compiling this book, my body became a home for my future daughter. I made my body suffer so much when I was anorexic, but ultimately it taught me what forgiveness means. After neglecting and hating it, it gave me the gift of becoming pregnant, as if it were answering an insult with a compliment. I was at a loss for words, partly because of joy and partly because of shame. This shame, however, quickly went away and turned into a feeling of self-compassion. As a result, I appreciated every bout of nausea, all the stiffness and dizziness, along with every moment of fatigue that punctuated my magnificent pregnancy.

I became Jeanne's mother, which forced me to radically rethink my definition of success. Although our society puts a lot of emphasis on personal fame, popularity, power, and money, Jeanne has made me understand that success is not something bestowed from the outside, but the path we choose for ourselves. Success is a state of mind, a balanced self-awareness, a fulfilled soul, a pure intention, a duty, a wound that's been healed, a labour of love that you bring to fruition for all the right reasons. This awareness has helped me conceive and write each of these pages with the utmost humility and for the sole purpose of celebrating food and our well-being.

As for me and Alex, we've learned to become better parents, creators, and partners, all of which enabled us to become a stronger couple. With all our obvious but none-theless enriching imperfections, we've broken up and gotten back together a couple of times.

This book is full of love, ideas, flavours, truths, simplicity, and inspiration. It represents many days devoted to cooking, eating, laughing, crying, succeeding, and then photographing delicious dishes. It's the result of many hours spent sitting in front of my screen, while Jeanne was sleeping, trying to write down each recipe as clearly as possible. It's the answer to all my anxieties, which which were telling me I'd never get there on account of exhaustion. It's one of my biggest achievements, as I define them.

From my family to yours.

—

MARILOU

CONTENTS

The merit of a human being lies in his knowledge and deeds, and not in the colour of his skin or his religion.

KHALIL GIBRAN

Categories

GIFT

Recipes bearing the seal *gift* were all conceived to thank those we love. Whether you're offering a birthday gift, thanking a host or hostess, or commemorating a retirement with a special treat, every reason is a good one to pamper the people you care about.

ECONOMICAL

Recipes bearing the seal *economical* require few ingredients, most of which are staples that you likely already have in your fridge or pantry.

INDULGENT

Recipes bearing the seal *indulgent* will be especially enticing to those who enjoy a little extravagance! They are richer in fat and sugar, sometimes breaded or fried, and always delicious. Some recipes use ingredients that are slightly more expensive but are easily adaptable with less costly components.

Recipes bearing the seal *entertaining* were created to make your job as host or hostess run smoothly, with delectable dishes to please even the most discerning palates! From soups to desserts, this category will allow you to plan the perfect menu.

QUICK & EASY

Recipes bearing the seal *quick & easy* take only 30 minutes, including preparation and cooking time. In just half an hour, you'll have a full family meal on the table and ready to eat — ideal for any weeknight.

GLUTEN FREE

Recipes bearing the seal *gluten free* are free of wheat or wheat products. Gluten is found in wheat and other grains, and can affect those with celiac disease or non-celiac gluten sensitivities. Use the BROW acronym to remember these grains: barley, rye, oats (unless certified gluten free), and wheat. (Triticale can also cause sensitivity.) Since the recipes in this book are almost exclusively made with simple, fresh ingredients, you probably won't encounter any gluten in this category; however, certain spice mixes, extracts, flavourings, and artificial colourings may contain trace elements of gluten, so be sure to check the ingredients on the labels of the products you are using or consult the company.

LACTOSE FREE

Recipes bearing the seal *lactose free* are free of dairy products, except for Parmesan cheese and butter, since firm or extra-firm cheeses generally don't affect people who are lactose intolerant. Certain recipes made with Greek yogurt don't have this seal, but if you have lactose intolerance and wish to try these recipes, lactose-free Greek yogurt is available in most supermarkets.

VEGETARIAN

Recipes bearing the seal *vegetarian* don't contain any meat, but do follow the lacto-ovo vegetarian philosophy. These recipes may contain eggs, honey, milk, or milk products. If you're a vegan, not to worry! It's easy to substitute ingredients: replace mayonnaise with vegan mayo, and yogurt with soy or nut yogurt. For an egg substitute, simply combine 1 teaspoon ground flaxseed with 1 tablespoon water, which will give the gooey texture and consistency of egg whites — it works like magic! I adore chicken broth, but soups are so easy to make vegan: just use a tasty vegetable broth instead.

HIS CHOICE

Recipes bearing the seal *his choice* have been specially curated by Alex — they're his absolute favourites. Trust me, if you need Alex to do you a favour, just whip up one of these dishes and he won't be able to say no!

Each recipe is accompanied by a symbol that indicates:

PREPARATION
TIME

COOKING
TIME

REST
TIME

MENU
IDEAS

I've always loved recipe books that read like novels.

At night, when other people might count sheep to fall asleep, I dream up recipes in my head. As strange as that might sound, it truly calms and comforts me.

I love thinking about the marriage of flavours or how I'll set my table to highlight my dishes and the look on the faces of my guests.

So here are a few ideas that I hope will help you to plan the meals you'll host, whether they be casual get-togethers or more formal sit-down dinners.

SUMMER MENU

APPETIZER

Cold avocado, mango & cucumber soup
with Nordic shrimp
page 140

MAIN

Tuna spring rolls with cashew dipping sauce
page 170

SIDE

Orzo with asparagus, lemon & Parmesan
page 249

DESSERT

Mascarpone, lemon & honey sorbet
page 288

ECONOMICAL MENU

APPETIZER

Cream of chickpea, curry & bacon soup
page 132

MAIN

Creamy tuna linguine
page 216

DESSERT

Blueberry & banana clafoutis
page 283

ENTERTAINING

CHIC MENU

AMUSE-BOUCHE

Homemade dukkah & olive oil dip

page 75

APPETIZER

Stracciatella (Italian egg soup) or
Rockefeller-style butterfly shrimp

page 128 or 174

MAIN

Barley risotto with tomatoes, duck
confit & bocconcini

page 232

DESSERT

Vanilla crème brûlée

page 280

VEGETARIAN MENU

APPETIZER

Leek, celery & lettuce soup with
express goat cheese gnocchi

page 142

MAIN

Vegetarian lasagna tart

page 261

SIDE

Green salad and vinaigrette bar

page 109

DESSERT

Cashew chocolate mousse

page 290

INDULGENT MENU

APPETIZER

Selection of snail crostini

pages 166 to 169

MAIN

Beef blade roast with root
vegetables & herb anchoïade

page 208

DESSERT

Giant chocolate chip & marshmallow
cookie casserole

page 293

MEATLOVER'S MENU

APPETIZER

Beef carpaccio with arugula vinaigrette &
Parmesan whipped cream

page 196

MAIN

Ribs with homemade barbecue sauce

page 204

SIDE

Portobellos stuffed with goat cheese

page 251

DESSERT

Double chocolate & maple
poor man's pudding

page 275

CHAPTER

No. 1

—

BREAKFAST &
BRUNCH

RICOTTA WAFFLES

RECIPE ON PAGE 32

I've categorized this recipe as quick & easy because you can prepare the waffles
on the weekend and simply pop them into the toaster on weekday mornings — they're
just as good reheated. Here are two topping ideas, keeping in mind that these waffles
are equally delicious when eaten with a bit of yogurt, fresh fruit, and chocolate,
as pictured on the cover page.

RICOTTA WAFFLES

BEST BEFORE

Serve immediately or freeze. The toppings will keep for 2 days in the fridge.

CATEGORIES

Indulgent · Entertaining · Quick & easy · Vegetarian

INGREDIENTS

1 cup milk

1 cup ricotta cheese

¼ cup butter, melted

4 eggs

1 tbsp lemon juice

1 tsp vanilla extract

¼ cup sugar

DRY INGREDIENTS

2 cups all-purpose flour

2 tsp baking powder

½ tsp baking soda

A pinch of salt

STEPS

1 Preheat the waffle iron.

2 In a bowl, combine the dry ingredients. Set aside.

3 In another bowl, whisk together the milk, ricotta, butter, eggs, lemon juice, vanilla, and sugar. Add the dry ingredients, and stir well.

4 Drop about ⅓ cup of the batter into the middle of the hot waffle iron, and close the lid tightly.

5 Cook for 2 to 3 minutes. Place the cooked waffles on a plate in the oven to keep them warm and repeat step 4 until the batter is used up.

YOGURT & PECAN TOPPING

INGREDIENTS

¾ cup plain yogurt

¼ cup brown sugar

¼ cup pecans, chopped

STEPS

1 In a bowl, beat together the yogurt and brown sugar.

2 Stir in the pecans, and serve.

CHOCOLATE & BACON TOPPING

INGREDIENTS

4 strips bacon, finely chopped

½ cup 35% cream

3 ½ oz dark (50%) chocolate, roughly chopped

STEPS

1 In a dry pan, fry the bacon until cooked through; drain the grease. Set the bacon aside to cool.

2 Meanwhile, heat the cream in a small pot. Remove from heat, and add the chocolate. Once the chocolate has melted, whip the mixture until smooth and creamy.

3 Stir in the bacon, and serve.

TIP

Prepare the batter the night before, and make the waffles the next morning.

My husband isn't really in the habit of tasting my sweet recipes anymore, since being diagnosed with diabetes. However, he made an exception for this one, which he had to force himself to stop eating or he'd have had the whole jar. For days afterward, he kept telling me how he dreamed of diving into a wading pool of cookie dough butter, mouth wide open. I was dying of laughter.

This recipe is brilliant as a host or hostess gift, or simply placed in the middle of the table for brunch. Try it on croissants, or on the ricotta waffles on page 32. I promise you'll thank the pregnant woman I was when I conceived of this recipe in the middle of the night.

QUANTITY : *1 ½ cups* · 🥄 10 MIN · *Freezes well.*

COOKIE DOUGH BUTTER

BEST BEFORE
Keeps for a few days at room temperature, or a few months in the fridge.

CATEGORIES
Gift · Entertaining · Quick & easy · Lactose free · Vegetarian

INGREDIENTS

3 tbsp water

¼ cup brown sugar

½ cup butter, at room temperature

1 tsp vanilla extract

½ cup icing sugar

3 tbsp all-purpose flour

¼ cup peanut butter

½ cup chocolate chips

STEPS

1 In a bowl, whisk together the water and brown sugar until all the sugar has dissolved. Transfer the mixture to a food processor, and add the remaining ingredients, with the exception of the chocolate chips. Process until smooth.

2 Transfer the mixture to a bowl, add the chocolate chips, and stir well. Serve immediately or store the spread in a sealed container in the fridge.

THIN CRÊPE CAKE WITH RASPBERRY TOPPING

HIS
CHOICE

BEST BEFORE - *Keeps for up to 48 hours in the fridge.*

CATEGORIES - *Indulgent · Entertaining · Vegetarian*

INGREDIENTS

FOR THE CRÊPES

6 eggs

½ cup sugar

1 tsp vanilla extract

3 ½ cups milk

3 cups all-purpose flour

Pinch of salt

Butter, for cooking

FOR THE RASPBERRY TOPPING

3 pints of raspberries

2 tubs (1 lb) mascarpone

¼ cup sugar

FOR THE WHIPPED CREAM

½ cup 35% cream

2 tbsp sugar

STEPS

1 In a large bowl, whisk together the eggs, sugar, and vanilla. Add the milk, flour, and salt, and stir until smooth. Set aside.

2 Lightly butter a 9-inch non-stick pan and cook the crêpes, one at a time, until they're nicely golden brown. Pile the crepes onto a plate and let them cool.

3 Set aside 1 pint of raspberries for decoration. In a bowl, combine the remaining raspberries with the mascarpone and sugar. Using a masher, mash until well blended. Set aside.

4 In another bowl, combine the cream and sugar and whip until stiff peaks form. Set aside.

5 Place 1 crêpe in the centre of a serving platter. Spread a fine layer of raspberry topping over top. Cover with another crêpe. Repeat until all of the crêpes are used and you have a stack resembling a cake. Cover the top with whipped cream, decorate with raspberries, and serve.

TIP

You can just as easily prepare the crêpes and toppings the night before, as well as assemble the cake a few hours in advance. Simply keep the cake in the fridge until it's time to serve.

A friend told me about birchermüesli, a recipe created by a Zürich physician during the Second World War to keep children well nourished. She discovered this marvellous dish while travelling in Switzerland. I thought it would be a fun challenge to adapt the recipe using ingredients that are easy to find in North America.

BEST BEFORE - *Keeps for 2 to 3 days in the fridge.*

CATEGORIES - *Economical · Lactose free · Vegetarian*

STEPS

1 The night before, combine all the birchermüesli ingredients in a bowl, cover, and set aside in the fridge. The "steeping" time is necessary so the flakes will be tender when ready to serve.

2 In the morning, combine all of the topping ingredients in a bowl, and serve with the birchermüesli.

INGREDIENTS

FOR THE BIRCHERMÜESLI

¾ cup quick-cooking oats

¼ cup whole buckwheat flakes (or barley, wheat, rye, etc.)

½ cup milk of your choice (almond, rice, soy, coconut, etc.)

½ cup store-bought pear or nectar juice

¼ cup golden raisins

2 tbsp maple syrup

A pinch of fleur de sel

FOR THE TOPPING

1 pear, cored and grated or finely chopped

A handful of seedless grapes, halved

A pinch of ground cinnamon

1 tsp honey, or more to taste

QUANTITY : *1–2 servings* · 🥄 5 MIN · ☾ 6 H MINIMUM · *Doesn't freeze well.*

PEAR & GRAPE BIRCHERMÜESLI

QUINOA, VEGETABLE & POACHED EGG BOWL WITH SPICED SAUCE

BEST BEFORE

Serve immediately, or store the ingredients separately in the fridge for up to 2 days.

CATEGORIES

Economical · Gluten free · Vegetarian

When I was pregnant but didn't know it yet, there was a week I went crazy for veggies. I even craved them first thing in the morning, so I came up with this bowl of quinoa with veggies, topped off with a poached egg, with a nice, runny yolk. Pure bliss! I know it sounds weird (maybe because it is a little), but you have to trust me and try it. It's so yummy you'll forget that you're chowing down on vegetables between sips of coffee.

It's also a great dish to serve for a late brunch.

CONTINUED ON PAGE 42

CONTINUED FROM PAGE 41

STEPS

1 In a bowl, combine all the sauce ingredients, and set aside in the fridge.

2 In a large pan, over medium-high heat, heat the olive oil. Sauté the carrots for 2 minutes, then add the zucchini. Sauté for another 2 minutes. Add the remaining vegetables, then cook for a further 2 minutes. Season to taste.

3 Reheat the quinoa, and serve garnished with vegetables, avocado quarters, and poached eggs. Pour sauce over everything.

INGREDIENTS

1 cup quinoa, cooked

1 avocado, quartered

Juice of ½ lime or ½ lemon, to sprinkle over avocado

2 eggs, poached (see tip below)

FOR THE VEGETABLES

1 tbsp olive oil

1 carrot, finely sliced

1 zucchini, cut into rounds

½ cup cherry tomatoes, halved

1 tsp curry powder

1 tbsp honey

2 tbsp finely chopped fresh basil

Salt and pepper, to taste

FOR THE SAUCE

2 tbsp mayonnaise

2 tbsp plain yogurt

½ tsp sweet paprika

1 tbsp honey

TIP

To make perfect poached eggs: Bring a pot of water to boil and add 1 tbsp of vinegar per poached egg. Reduce the heat to a simmer. Using a spoon, gently stir the water to create a whirlpool, then break an egg into it. Repeat with the remaining eggs. Cook for 3 ½ minutes, drain with a slotted spoon, and serve. Remember that the fresher the eggs, the better the result.

MORNING BROWNIE

RECIPE ON PAGE 46

MORNING BROWNIE

PHOTO ON PAGE 44

BEST BEFORE - *Keeps for 1 week in the fridge.*

CATEGORIES - *Gift · Lactose free · Entertaining · Vegetarian*

I'm not sure I really have the right to call this a brownie since
the texture is not at all what one would expect; the taste,
on the other hand, is just ... wow!

This recipe is definitely one of my favourites, and I say this
while fully acknowledging the giant portion I ate all by
myself in under two days.

QUANTITY : *16 squares* · ⚏ 15 MIN · 🕐 35 MIN · *Freezes well.*

INGREDIENTS

10 ½ oz plain silken tofu

1 ripe avocado, stoned, peeled, and sliced

½ cup store-bought unsweetened applesauce

½ cup maple syrup

*2 tbsp almond, soy, or peanut butter (or nut butter of
your choice)*

1 ½ cups whole-wheat flour (or all-purpose flour)

1 tsp baking powder

½ cup cocoa powder

1 cup dark chocolate chips

1 cup walnuts, roughly chopped

STEPS

1   Preheat the oven to 350°F, with the rack in
centre position. Line a 9-inch square baking pan
with parchment paper, and set aside.

2   In a bowl, combine the tofu, avocado, applesauce,
maple syrup, and nut butter. Using an electric mixer,
beat until smooth.

3   Add the flour, baking powder, and cocoa powder and,
using a wooden spoon, stir well.

4   Add the chocolate chips and walnuts, and stir well.
Transfer the batter to the baking pan, and bake for 30 minutes.
Let the brownies cool completely in the pan before
cutting into squares. Serve.

1 cup all-purpose flour

¾ cup whole-wheat flour

¼ cup chia seeds

1 tsp baking powder

½ tsp baking soda

¼ tsp salt

FOR THE WET INGREDIENTS

2 eggs

¼ cup vegetable oil

1 cup puréed sweet potato (see tip below)

½ cup water

½ cup brown sugar

1 tsp vanilla extract

1 ½ cups cranberries (fresh or frozen)

STEPS

1 Preheat the oven to 350°F, with the rack in centre position. Butter a 5-inch × 9-inch loaf pan and set aside.

2 In a bowl, combine all the dry ingredients. Set aside.

3 In another bowl, whisk together all the wet ingredients, with the exception of the cranberries.

4 Add the dry ingredients to the wet ingredients, and stir well. Fold in the cranberries. Transfer the mixture to the loaf pan.

5 Bake for 1 hour, or until a toothpick inserted in the middle of the loaf comes out clean.

6 Let cool in the loaf pan for a minimum of 15 minutes before serving.

TIP

To make the sweet potato purée, peel a sweet potato, and then cut into 1 cm slices. Put the slices into a pot, cover with water, and bring to a boil. Simmer for 15 minutes, drain, and process in a food processer, or mash with a masher, until smooth. Measure out the desired quantity.

SWEET POTATO, CHIA & CRANBERRY LOAF

BEST BEFORE
Keeps for 2 to 3 days in a sealed container at room temperature, or 3 to 4 days in the fridge.

CATEGORIES
Gift · Economical · Entertaining · Lactose free · Vegetarian

BREAKFAST BAGEL, TWO WAYS

BEST BEFORE   -   *Serve immediately.*

CATEGORIES   -   *Economical · Indulgent · Quick & easy*

I've always dreamed of creating a recipe that mimics the way interior design magazines show two almost identical rooms, composed of different items. One room is assembled using economical materials; in the other room, price is no object. I amuse myself trying to decide which is which, just like the girl who completes the "Are you a good best friend?" questionnaire in her favourite magazine.

Inspired by this concept, I created two bagels: one express and one deluxe. And by the way, in this recipe you'll also discover how to make the world's best scrambled eggs. *Bon appétit!*

CONTINUED ON PAGE 52

QUANTITY : *1 bagel* · 🥄 5 MIN · 🕐 10 MIN · *Doesn't freeze well.*

DELUXE VERSION

INGREDIENTS

1 tsp butter

1 slice prosciutto, finely chopped

½ cup baby spinach

1 tbsp cream cheese

1 bagel, split in half

FOR THE BEST SCRAMBLED EGGS
IN THE WORLD

1 egg

1 tbsp minced chives

Salt and pepper, to taste

1 tsp butter

1 tsp 15% or 35% cream

STEPS

1 In a pan, melt the butter. Brown the prosciutto for 1 minute. Add the spinach and cream cheese, stir well, and set aside.

2 Toast the bagel in the toaster. Set aside.

3 In a small bowl, whisk together the egg and chives. Season.

4 In a small non-stick pan, melt the butter. Add the egg and cook, stirring constantly using a rubber spatula to prevent the egg from sticking to the pan.

5 Once the egg is cooked, remove the pan from the heat. Add the cream, and stir vigorously. The cream will stop the egg from cooking and provide a smooth and creamy texture. Season. Top the bagel with the egg and garnish with the spinach and prosciutto mixture. Serve.

QUANTITY : *1 bagel* · 🥄 5 MIN · 🕐 1 MIN · *Doesn't freeze well.*

EXPRESS VERSION

INGREDIENTS

1 bagel, split in half

1 tsp vegetable oil

1 egg

¼ cup shredded cheddar cheese

1 slice ham, finely chopped

⅓ cup baby spinach

¼ tsp onion powder

Salt and pepper, to taste

STEPS

1 Toast the bagel in the toaster. Set aside.

2 Grease the sides of a small microwave-safe bowl with the vegetable oil. Add the remaining ingredients, and stir well. Cook on High for 30 seconds in the microwave. Repeat. It's important to cook the eggs in two steps to avoid spillover.

3 Top the bagel with the omelette. Serve.

WAFFLE, JAM, HAM & CHEESE SANDWICHES

Sometimes, I pretend I'm Martin Picard (just saying the name of the founder of the luxurious restaurant Au Pied de Cochon makes my stomach rumble), and the result is recipes like this one. You'll see that having leftover homemade waffles (see recipe on page 32) in the freezer will make you want to use them anywhere you'd use bread — which is great because then I won't be alone in this regard. Have fun coming up with different waffle sandwich combos; it boosts morale.

BEST BEFORE - *Serve immediately.*

CATEGORIES - *Indulgent · Quick & easy*

INGREDIENTS

4 waffles (see recipe on page 32)

4 tbsp fig jam (or jam of your choice)

6 thin slices ham

1 cup shredded cheddar cheese

Maple syrup, to taste

STEPS

1   Toast the waffles in the toaster.
Top 2 waffles with jam, ham, and cheese.

2   Place under the broiler for a few minutes, until the cheese is nicely melted. Cover each sandwich with the remaining waffles, douse with maple syrup, and serve.

CHIA PUDDING WITH MANGO & COCONUT PURÉE

BEST BEFORE - *Keeps for 2 days in the fridge.*

CATEGORIES - *Quick & easy · Gluten free · Vegetarian*

INGREDIENTS

½ cup vanilla almond milk (or other milk)

½ cup coconut yogurt

1 cup chopped mango (fresh or frozen)

3 tbsp chia seeds

Shredded coconut, for serving

CHOICE OF FRUIT, FOR SERVING

Dragon fruit

Mango

Peach

Passion fruit

STEPS

1   In a food processor, combine all the ingredients, and process until smooth. You should still be able to see the chia seeds.

2   Transfer the mixture to a bowl, cover, and refrigerate overnight, or for a minimum of 4 hours, before serving.

3   Serve with the coconut and your fruits of choice.

This recipe is a life-saver for coffee lovers whose lives are so busy they always end up drinking their coffee cold. I decided to incorporate morning coffee into a breakfast dish. Aren't I a genius?
I think so.

CAFÉ LATTE OATMEAL

BEST BEFORE

Keeps for 2 to 3 days in the fridge.
If the mixture is too thick, thin it out with some almond milk.

CATEGORIES

Economical · Quick & easy · Lactose free · Vegetarian

INGREDIENTS

½ cup brewed coffee

3 tbsp honey (or maple syrup)

1 cup quick-cooking oats

¼ cup chopped almonds

1 cup vanilla almond milk

Bananas and/or blueberries, for serving

Dark chocolate shavings, for serving

STEPS

1   In a small pot, combine the coffee, honey, oats, almonds, and almond milk.

2   Bring to a boil, reduce the heat to low, and simmer for 1 to 2 minutes. Adjust the honey to taste, and serve with fruit and dark chocolate shavings.

HIS
CHOICE

CHAPTER

No.²

—

SNACKS &
SMALL BITES

HOMEMADE POPCORN

RECIPE ON PAGE 64

BEST BEFORE - *Keeps for 1 day.*

CATEGORIES - *Economical · Indulgent · Entertaining · Quick & easy*
Lactose free · Gluten free · Vegetarian

HOMEMADE POPCORN

PHOTO ON PAGE 62

Alex and I are the biggest popcorn fans of all time. For a while, we ate it every night, out of habit, and it quickly became boring. I totally stopped eating it — until the day I came up with a whole bunch of flavourings that could be prepared in seconds. I challenge you to not go crazy for these, like we did.

INGREDIENTS

3 tbsp canola oil (or coconut oil)
½ cup popcorn kernels

BARBECUE

INGREDIENTS

½ tsp smoked paprika
½ tsp sweet paprika
2 tsp sugar
½ tsp garlic powder
½ tsp salt
*1 tsp Worcestershire sauce combined
with 2 tbsp melted butter*

SUGAR & SPICE

INGREDIENTS

½ tsp salt
1 tsp ground cinnamon
1 tbsp sugar
2 tbsp melted butter

PARMESAN & ONION

INGREDIENTS

½ tsp salt

1 tsp onion powder

½ tsp mustard powder

¼ cup freshly grated Parmesan cheese

2 tbsp melted butter

SUMAC, PEPPER & CUMIN

INGREDIENTS

2 tsp ground sumac

½ tsp ground cumin

¼ tsp black pepper

¼ tsp salt

2 tbsp melted butter

STEPS

1   In a large pot, over high heat, heat the oil and 2 popcorn kernels. Once the kernels pop, remove the pot from the heat, and then add the remaining popcorn; it should form a single layer in the bottom of the pot. Cover the pot with the lid (important), and wait 30 seconds. I repeat: off the heat.

2   Put the pot back on the heat, and wait a few seconds. All the kernels should pop pretty much at the same time. To help the popcorn pop, gently shake the pot.

3   Remove the pot from heat, and remove the lid. Transfer the popcorn to a bowl. Set aside.

4   In a small bowl, combine all the dry ingredients of the flavour of your choice. Sprinkle over the popcorn.

5   Pour the melted butter (or the butter mixture) over the popcorn, and stir well. Serve.

This idea came to me when I was brainstorming indulgent gifts that are a little out of the ordinary. I promise it'll be a topic of conversation when you present your host with homemade marinated feta. It looks pretty, and it can jazz up lots of dishes, from bruschetta, to pasta, to savoury tarts, to salads. It's also yummy on its own, on bread.

Don't be afraid to bite into a pink peppercorn: they're delicious.

HOMEMADE MARINATED FETA

BEST BEFORE - *Keeps for about 1 month in the fridge.*

CATEGORIES - *Gift · Entertaining · Gluten free · Vegetarian*

SNACKS & SMALL BITES

INGREDIENTS

1 block (7 oz) of your favourite feta cheese, cubed

1 cup grapeseed oil

1 tbsp minced fresh chives

4 sprigs fresh thyme

2 tsp whole pink peppercorns

1 small hot pepper of your choice, minced

STEPS

1   Put the cubes of feta in a glass jar that comfortably holds 2 cups. Set aside.

2   In a bowl, combine the remaining ingredients, and stir well. Pour over the cheese in the jar, making sure that the cheese is completely covered. If it's not, add a bit more oil.

3   Cover and let marinate in the fridge for a minimum of 24 hours before offering as a gift or serving.

WARM CAJUN SHRIMP DIP

BEST BEFORE - *Keeps for 2 to 3 days in the fridge.*

CATEGORIES - *Indulgent · Entertaining · Gluten free*

INGREDIENTS

1 tbsp butter

1 yellow onion, minced

2 tomatoes, seeded and diced

1 cup Nordic shrimp, cooked

1 cup (half a 19 oz can) white beans, rinsed and drained

1 cup shredded mozzarella cheese

½ cup sour cream

1 to 2 tsp store-bought Cajun spice

Salt and pepper, to taste

STEPS

1   Preheat the oven to 400°F, with the rack in centre position.

2   In a pan, over medium heat, melt the butter. Add the onion, and cook for 5 minutes, or until soft.

3   Transfer the cooked onion to a food processor, along with the tomatoes and shrimp. Pulse just a few times, being careful to retain some texture. Transfer the mixture to a bowl. Set aside.

4   In the same food processing bowl, combine the white beans, cheese, sour cream, and spices and process until smooth. Add to the shrimp mixture, and stir well. Season.

5   Transfer to an oven-proof dish.

6   Bake for 30 minutes, or until heated through.

7   Finish under the broiler. Let cool for 5 minutes before serving.

TIP

Serve with fresh bread, chips, crackers, crudités, cheese, etc.

QUANTITY : *8 servings*

15 MIN · 35 MIN · 5 MIN · *Doesn't freeze well.*

ONION BHAJI (INDIAN FRITTERS)
WITH DATE SAUCE

In Indian restaurants, onion bhaji are served with tamarind sauce. Since tamarind can be hard to find at the grocery store, I tried to reproduce the flavour using dates. I must say, I succeeded. I hope you'll enjoy these as much as Alex, who's dubbed this recipe "one of the world's best."

HIS
CHOICE

BEST BEFORE

The uncooked mixture keeps for a few days in the fridge. If the onions begin to weep, add a little chickpea flour. You can cook the fritters in advance and reheat them in the oven. The sauce keeps for a few weeks in the fridge.

CATEGORIES

Entertaining · Lactose free · Gluten free · Vegetarian

INGREDIENTS

FOR THE SAUCE

4 Medjool dates, pitted

¾ cup water

2 tbsp apple cider vinegar

¼ tsp ground cumin

Salt and pepper, to taste

FOR THE FRITTERS

2 cups finely minced yellow onions

2 tbsp lime juice

½ tsp salt

2 tbsp chopped fresh cilantro

1 cup chickpea flour

½ cup water

2 tsp curry powder

½ tsp garlic powder

1 tsp Sriracha sauce

2 tsp baking soda

Black pepper, to taste

Vegetable oil, for cooking

STEPS

FOR THE SAUCE

1 In a pot, combine the dates and the water. Bring to a boil, reduce the heat, and simmer for 2 minutes. Stir in the remaining sauce ingredients. Remove from the heat. Using an immersion or regular blender, blend until smooth. Transfer to a bowl, and let cool completely in the fridge.

FOR THE FRITTERS

2 In a bowl, combine the onions, lime juice, and salt. Cover and refrigerate for 15 minutes, or until the onions begin to soften.

3 Add the remaining fritter ingredients, and stir well. Set aside.

4 Fill a non-stick pan with 1 cm of vegetable oil, and heat over medium heat. Drop batter by the tablespoonful into the hot oil and fry until golden brown, turning once. Drain on paper towel. Serve with the date sauce.

Before telling anyone that your chocolate muffins are made with carrots, zucchini, and spinach, make sure they try them first.

CHOCOLATE & CAMOUFLAGED VEGGIE MUFFINS

72

BEST BEFORE

Keeps for 2 to 3 days in a sealed container at room temperature, or 1 week in the fridge.

CATEGORIES - *Lactose free · Vegetarian*

SNACKS & SMALL BITES

INGREDIENTS

FOR THE WET INGREDIENTS

1 cup zucchini, cut into rounds

1 cup sweet potato, peeled and diced

1 cup carrots, peeled and cut into rounds

2 cups baby spinach

1 apple, cored and quartered

½ cup vegetable oil

2 eggs

1 cup brown sugar

FOR THE DRY INGREDIENTS

1 cup whole-wheat flour

1 cup all-purpose flour

½ cup cocao powder

1 tsp vanilla extract

2 tsp baking powder

Pinch of salt

STEPS

1   Preheat the oven to 350°F, with the rack in centre position. Line 18 muffin cups with paper liners. Set aside.

2   In a food processor, finely chop all the vegetables and the apple. Transfer to a big bowl, and stir in the remaining wet ingredients. Set aside.

3   In another bowl, combine all the dry ingredients. Add to the wet ingredients. Stir until just combined.

4   Divide batter evenly among the muffin cups. Bake for 30 minutes, or until a toothpick inserted in the centre comes out clean.

TIP

I recommend a combination of whole-wheat and all-purpose flour, but you can use only one of the two, if you like, provided the amount totals 2 cups.

Here's an appetizer that'll impress with its unique flavour. Serve with fresh bread.
It also makes a great host/hostess gift, offered alongside a nice bottle of olive oil.
Feel free to double, triple, or centuple the recipe.

HOMEMADE DUKKAH
& OLIVE OIL DIP

QUANTITY : *½ cup (or approximately 2 servings)* · 🥄 8 MIN · *Doesn't freeze well.*

BEST BEFORE

Keeps for a few weeks in the fridge, depending on the freshness of the ingredients.

CATEGORIES

Gift · Entertaining · Quick & easy · Lactose free · Gluten free · Vegetarian

INGREDIENTS

1 tsp fresh thyme leaves

½ tsp ground cumin

1 tbsp sesame seeds

3 tbsp finely chopped almonds

1 tsp balsamic vinegar

Zest of ½ lemon

⅓ cup good-quality olive oil

¼ tsp fleur de sel

Fresh bread, for serving

STEPS

1   In a small bowl, combine all the
ingredients, with the exception of the bread.
Transfer the mixture to a small plate, and
serve with pieces of fresh bread.

Most recipes for sesame crackers call for lots of corn syrup, or a candy thermometer, but I always prefer simple recipes made with few tools or modified ingredients.

This is an excellent recipe that's really easy to make. The crackers are a perfect base for spreading hummus, cheese, or sunflower seed dip (recipe on page 82).

BEST BEFORE

Keeps for a few weeks in a sealed container at room temperature.

CATEGORIES

Gift · Economical · Lactose free · Vegetarian

INGREDIENTS

½ cup sesame seeds

½ cup pumpkin seeds

½ cup sunflower seeds

½ cup all-purpose flour

¼ cup honey

¼ cup water

¼ cup olive oil

2 tbsp lime juice

½ tsp baking soda

½ tsp salt

STEPS

1   Preheat the oven to 325°F, with the rack in centre position. Line a baking sheet with parchment paper. Set aside.

2   In a bowl, combine all the ingredients.

3   Spread the mixture evenly on the baking sheet to form a 9-inch × 13-inch rectangle.

4   Bake for 30 to 40 minutes, or until golden brown. Cut into crackers immediately, and let cool.

SESAME & HONEY CRACKERS

QUANTITY : *20 crackers* · 🥄 10 MIN · 🕐 35 MIN · 🌙 5 MIN · *Freezes well.*

Alex judged me harshly when he saw this recipe. He found it dead boring, while I was in love with a masterpiece. So we compromised and included it in the book — *ha ha!*

This is *the* appetizer to impress and get your guests talking, especially at a picnic. It's both refreshing and tasty.

MELON BITES WITH PROSCIUTTO, NUTS & CILANTRO

BEST BEFORE - *Keeps for 2 to 3 days in the fridge.*

CATEGORIES - *Entertaining · Quick & easy · Lactose free · Gluten free*

INGREDIENTS

20 cubes honeydew melon

20 cubes watermelon

20 cubes cantaloupe

FOR THE TOPPING

6 slices prosciutto (or bacon)

¼ cup pecans, roughly chopped

¼ cup vegetable oil (I used grapeseed oil)

1 tbsp lime juice

3 tbsp chopped fresh cilantro

½ tsp ground Aleppo pepper (or Espelette pepper)

STEPS

1   Arrange the melon cubes on a serving plate, or on parchment paper placed in the middle of the table. Set aside.

2   In the microwave on High, cook the prosciutto slices on paper towel for 4 minutes, or until crispy. Chop the cooked prosciutto, then add it to a bowl, along with the remaining topping ingredients. Stir well.

3   Sprinkle the mixture over the melon cubes. Serve.

TIP

Replace a few melon cubes with cubes of marinated feta (see recipe on page 67) or avocado.

I chose to make cute mini-balls, but this recipe is equally delicious, and perhaps even more impressive, made as one mega-ball to share.

BRUSCHETTA-FLAVOURED CHEESEBALLS

BEST BEFORE - *Keeps for 2 to 3 days in the fridge.*

CATEGORIES - *Gift · Indulgent · Entertaining*

INGREDIENTS

Crostini, to serve

FOR THE CHEESE

6 strips bacon, cooked and chopped

2 Italian tomatoes, seeded and diced

¼ cup chopped fresh basil

2 tbsp chopped fresh oregano

¼ cup chopped fresh chives

½ cup Italian breadcrumbs

Salt and pepper, to taste

1 cup shredded mozzarella cheese

½ cup goat cheese

2 tbsp olive oil

FOR THE COATING

4 strips bacon, cooked and chopped

2 tsp sweet paprika

¼ cup chopped fresh chives

¼ cup chopped fresh parsley

STEPS

1 In a food processor, combine all the cheese ingredients, with the exception of the mozzarella, goat cheese, and olive oil, and pulse until it reaches a grainy texture.

2 Add the three missing ingredients, and pulse just to combine. Transfer the mixture to a bowl, cover, and refrigerate for a minimum of 30 minutes.

3 In a shallow bowl, combine all the coating ingredients. Set aside.

4 With slightly moistened hands, roll into cheese balls (about ¾ inches in diameter each) or one mega-ball. Roll in the coating mixture until completely covered. Serve with crostini.

SUNFLOWER SEED DIP

BEST BEFORE - *Keeps for 1 week in the fridge.*

CATEGORIES - *Gift · Economical · Quick & easy · Gluten free · Vegetarian*

INGREDIENTS

1 tbsp olive oil

2 green onions, minced

1 clove chopped garlic

1 tsp ground cumin

1 cup sunflower seeds

¾ cup plain yogurt

1 tbsp soy sauce (or tamari)

¼ cup fresh parsley

Juice of ½ lemon

Salt and pepper, to taste

STEPS

1   In a small pan, over medium heat, heat the olive oil.
Add the green onions and garlic, and cook for 3 to 4 minutes,
or until softened. Add the cumin, and stir well.
Transfer to a food processor.

2   Add the remaining ingredients, and process until smooth.
Adjust the seasoning, cover, and refrigerate before serving.

QUANTITY : *6 bars* · 🥄 10 MIN · ☾ 15 MIN · *Freezes well.*

GUIDE TO RAW BARS

BEST BEFORE

Keeps for a few weeks in the fridge.

CATEGORIES

Gift · Economical · Quick & easy · Lactose free · Gluten free · Vegetarian

1 CUP DATES

Medjool dates (or regular dates), pitted

1 CUP DRIED FRUIT,
TO TASTE

*Apricots, Sultana raisins, Golden raisins,
Cranberries, Apples, Figs*

½ CUP SEEDS,
TO TASTE

*Sunflower seeds, Pumpkin seeds,
Sesame seeds, Soy Nuts*

½ CUP NUTS,
TO TASTE
(SEE TIP BELOW FOR ALLERGIES)

*Almonds, Cashews, Walnuts, Pecans, Hazelnuts,
Shredded coconut, Peanuts*

1 TBSP BUTTER,
TO TASTE

*Peanut butter, Pecan butter, Chocolate spread,
Pea butter, Coconut oil*

¼ CUP SUPERFOOD,
TO TASTE

*Black or red chia seeds, Flaxseeds,
Hemp hearts*

SEASONING,
TO TASTE (OPTIONAL)

*½ tsp ground cinnamon, 1 tbsp cocoa powder,
Zest of ½ orange, 2 ground cardamom pods*

CONTINUED ON PAGE 86

CONTINUED FROM PAGE 85

STEPS

1   Line a 9-inch × 5-inch loaf pan with
plastic wrap. Set aside.

2   In a food processor, combine the dates,
dried fruit, butter, superfood, and seasoning, and
process until a paste is formed.

3   Add the seeds and the nuts. Pulse a few times,
being careful to keep some chunks.

4   Press the mixture into the bottom
of the loaf pan, until compact. Cover and
refrigerate for 1 hour.

5   Remove from the loaf pan, and cut into bars.
Keep the bars in a sealed container in the fridge,
separated by parchment paper.

TIP

To make nut-free, simply replace the nuts with an equal amount of seeds.

CHAPTER

No.³

—

LUNCH & SALADS

When it comes to preparing a "no fuss, no muss" meal, most people's first instinct is to serve a platter of charcuterie and cheese to their guests. I wanted to take this idea a step further by coming up with self-serve accompaniments to offer along with ingredients usually bought at the grocery store.

I encourage you to cover your entire table with parchment paper and set out the whole meal. Eat it with your fingers, laugh, and then simply crumple up the parchment paper when you're done eating and rejoice that there are no dishes to wash (or hardly any)!

LUNCH ON THE TABLE

APPLE, ONION & RAISIN CHUTNEY, PAGE 93
FIG, TOMATO & BASIL TOPPING, PAGE 94
APRICOT & PECAN TOPPING, PAGE 95
RICOTTA & HERB ROLLS, PAGE 97
HARD, SEMI-HARD & SOFT CHEESES, TO TASTE
SLICED COLD CUTS, TO TASTE
RILLETTES, TERRINES, OR PÂTÉS, TO TASTE
FRESH CHEESES, TO TASTE

CONTINUED ON PAGES 92 TO 97

APPLE, ONION & RAISIN CHUTNEY

QUANTITY : *1 cup* · 🥄 5 MIN · 🕐 20 MIN · ☾ 1 H · *Doesn't freeze well.*

BEST BEFORE - *Keeps for 2 weeks in the fridge.*

CATEGORIES - *Entertaining · Lactose free · Gluten free · Vegetarian*

INGREDIENTS

1 tbsp butter

1 cup minced red onion

1 McIntosh apple, peeled, cored, and finely diced

¼ cup raisins

2 tbsp brown sugar

1 tbsp apple cider vinegar

STEPS

1 In a small pot, over medium heat, melt the butter. Sauté the onion for 10 minutes, stirring occasionally, until nicely browned.

2 Stir in the remaining ingredients, cover with a lid, reduce the heat to low, and continue cooking for 8 minutes. Transfer to a bowl, and let cool slightly, then cover and cool completely in the fridge.

3 Serve with cold cuts.

FIG, TOMATO
& BASIL TOPPING

BEST BEFORE - *Serve immediately.*

CATEGORIES - *Entertaining · Quick & easy · Lactose free · Gluten free · Vegetarian*

INGREDIENTS

2 fresh figs, quartered

½ cup cherry tomatoes, quartered

3 or 4 fresh basil leaves, chopped

1 tsp sugar

1 tsp balsamic vinegar

1 tbsp olive oil

½ tsp fleur de sel

STEPS

1   Combine all the ingredients in a bowl, and serve on the fresh cheese of your choice.

APRICOT & PECAN TOPPING

BEST BEFORE - *Keeps for 2 to 3 days in the fridge.*

CATEGORIES - *Entertaining · Quick & easy · Lactose free · Gluten free · Vegetarian*

INGREDIENTS

*2 apricots, peaches, or nectarines, stoned
and quartered*

½ cup pecans or walnuts (or both)

1 tbsp butter

2 tbsp honey

1 tsp lemon juice

STEPS

1   In a pot, over medium-high heat, melt the butter, and then brown the apricots and nuts for 2 to 3 minutes.

2   Stir in the honey and lemon juice. Serve with cheese.

I just love these rolls, which in addition to being really delicious, give me
a sense of pride when I see them rising in the oven. I make them in
muffin pans for the perfect size.

Personally, I love rosemary, but I know it's not a herb everyone appreciates.
Therefore, I've suggested a few substitutions in the list of ingredients.

RICOTTA & HERB ROLLS

HIS
CHOICE

QUANTITY : *12 rolls* · 🥄 15 MIN · 🕐 15 MIN · ☾ 2 H 30 · *Freezes well.*

BEST BEFORE

*Keeps for 1 to 2 days at room
temperature.*

CATEGORIES

*Indulgent · Entertaining ·
Vegetarian*

INGREDIENTS

¾ cup water

1 packet (¼ oz) or 2 tsp quick-rising yeast

1 tbsp sugar

1 tsp salt

½ cup ricotta cheese

*1 tbsp chopped fresh rosemary (or thyme,
    oregano, sage)*

2 ¼ cups all-purpose flour

STEPS

1   Heat the water in the microwave on
    High for 30 seconds, or until just warm.

2   In a bowl, stir together all the ingredients
    until a ball of dough forms. Turn the
    dough out onto a clean work surface and
    vigorously knead for 5 minutes, or until
    smooth. Transfer to a bowl.

3   Cover with plastic wrap, and let rise
    in a warm place for about 2 hours (for
    example, in a closed oven with the oven
    light on).

4   Turn the dough out onto a clean work
    surface and knead again for 1 minute.
    Divide into 12 even balls. Transfer the
    balls to a greased 12-cup muffin pan.
    Set aside for 30 minutes in a warm place
    to rise.

5   Preheat the oven to 400°F. If you put
    your dough in the oven to rise, don't
    forget to take it out before this step.

6   Bake for 15 minutes.

LUNCH & SALADS

TIP

*The first step is important because warm water activates the yeast in the dough,
ensuring that the rolls rise properly.*

TROUT & POPCORN SALAD
WITH CREAMY APPLE DRESSING

BEST BEFORE - *The dressing keeps for 2 to 3 weeks in the fridge.*

CATEGORIES - *Quick & easy · Lactose free · Gluten free*

INGREDIENTS

Salt and pepper, to taste

14 oz fresh trout fillet, cut in half

1 tbsp olive oil

2 cups mesclun salad mix

4 Lebanese cucumbers, cut into rounds

A few cherry tomatoes, halved

1 ½ cups plain or seasoned popcorn (see homemade popcorn recipe on page 64)

FOR THE DRESSING

2 tbsp mayonnaise

2 tbsp unsweetened applesauce, homemade or store-bought

1 tbsp rice vinegar

2 tsp Dijon mustard

Salt and pepper, to taste

STEPS

1 In a bowl, combine all the dressing ingredients. Set aside.

2 Season the trout generously. In a pan, over high heat, heat the olive oil. Sear the trout for 2 minutes per side. Remove the skin and set aside.

3 In a salad bowl, combine the lettuce, cucumbers, and tomatoes. Add the popcorn, and toss to combine. Top with the trout. Drizzle with the dressing.

MUSHROOM & PISTACHIO PESTO ON TOAST

QUANTITY : *4 tarts* · 🥄 10 MIN · 🕐 5 MIN · *Doesn't freeze well.*

BEST BEFORE - *Keep for 1 week in the fridge.*
CATEGORIES - *Lactose free · Vegetarian*

INGREDIENTS

4 slices bread, or to taste
Alfalfa or other leafy greens, for serving

FOR THE PESTO

⅓ cup unsalted shelled pistachios
½ cup fresh parsley
¼ cup olive oil
½ clove garlic, chopped
1 tsp lemon juice
1 tbsp water
Salt and pepper, to taste

FOR THE MUSHROOMS

1 tbsp butter
1 package (8 oz) white mushrooms, quartered
Juice of ½ lemon
1 tbsp maple syrup
Salt and pepper, to taste

STEPS

1   In a food processor, combine all the pesto ingredients, and process until smooth. Set aside.

2   In a pan, over high heat, melt the butter. Sauté the mushrooms until browned. Stir in the lemon juice and maple syrup. Season and set aside.

3   Toast the bread, and slather generously with pesto. Top with the mushrooms and greens, and serve.

QUANTITY : *4 servings* · 5 MIN · *Doesn't freeze well.*

LOBSTER, QUINOA & FRESH HERB SALAD

102

BEST BEFORE - *Keeps for 2 to 3 days in the fridge.*
CATEGORIES - *Quick & easy · Lactose free · Gluten free*

INGREDIENTS

2 cups lobster meat
¼ cup mayonnaise
Juice of ½ lemon
1 tbsp chopped fresh tarragon
1 to 2 tbsp chopped fresh basil
½ cup red and white quinoa
1 green onion, minced
Salt and pepper, to taste
Boston lettuce leaves, for serving
Bread, for serving

STEPS

1   In a bowl, combine all the ingredients, with the exception of the lettuce and the bread, and stir well. Adjust the seasoning to taste. Serve with the lettuce and bread.

Avocado on toast is trendy so you're probably reading this and thinking I'm not very original, or I think I'm Gwyneth Paltrow, but wait! I honestly believe I've brought avocado on toast to a whole new level with these delicious and original toppings.

This is the kind of dish that I can make quickly and easily when I'm alone and hungry, or when I've got girlfriends coming over for lunch and I want to impress them. Enjoy!

AVOCADO ON TOAST, SIX WAYS

BEST BEFORE - *Serve immediately.*

CATEGORIES - *Economical · Quick & easy · Lactose free · Vegetarian*

QUANTITY : *2 servings* · 🥄 5 MIN · 🕐 2 MIN · *Doesn't freeze well.*

CLASSIC AVOCADO

INGREDIENTS

2 slices bread

2 tsp mayonnaise (or veganaise)

1 ripe avocado, stoned, peeled, and sliced or mashed

Fleur de sel

STEPS

1   Toast the bread slices. Spread with mayonnaise, top with avocado, and season with fleur de sel.

AVOCADO, CAPERS & SARDINES

INGREDIENTS

2 slices bread

2 tsp mayonnaise (or veganaise)

1 ripe avocado, stoned, peeled, and sliced or mashed

2 tsp capers, drained and chopped

1 can (4 oz) sardine fillets, drained

STEPS

1   Toast the bread slices. Spread with mayonnaise, and top with avocado, capers, and sardines.

CONTINUED ON PAGE 106

CONTINUED FROM PAGE 105

AVOCADO, SPICY MAYONNAISE & CILANTRO

INGREDIENTS

1 tsp sesame seeds

2 slices bread

2 tsp mayonnaise (or veganaise)

3 ½ tsp Sriracha sauce

1 ripe avocado, stoned, peeled, and sliced or mashed

1 tbsp chopped fresh cilantro

STEPS

1 In a dry pan, over medium heat, toast the sesame seeds until golden. Set aside.

2 Toast the bread slices. Set aside.

3 In another bowl, combine the mayonnaise and Sriracha. Spread on the toast. Top with avocado, cilantro, and the toasted sesame seeds.

AVOCADO, HARD-BOILED EGGS & DILL

INGREDIENTS

2 eggs

2 slices bread

1 ripe avocado, stoned, peeled, and sliced or mashed

1 tbsp chopped fresh dill

Fleur de sel

STEPS

1 Put the eggs in a pot, and cover with water. Bring to a boil, cover the pot with a lid, and remove from the heat. Set aside for 10 to 12 minutes.

2 Transfer the eggs to a bowl of very cold water. Peel the eggs, then slice them. Set aside.

3 Toast the bread slices. Top with avocado, sliced eggs, and dill. Season with fleur de sel and serve.

AVOCADO, LIME & FETA

INGREDIENTS

2 slices bread

*1 ripe avocado, stoned, peeled, and sliced
    or mashed*

2 tbsp crumbled feta cheese

Juice of ½ lime

Freshly ground black pepper

STEPS

1 Toast the bread slices. Top with avocado
   and feta cheese. Drizzle with lime juice,
   and season with pepper. Serve.

AVOCADO, STRAWBERRY & SMOKED SALMON

INGREDIENTS

2 slices bread

3 or 4 slices smoked salmon

*1 ripe avocado, stoned, peeled, and sliced
    or mashed*

4 strawberries, hulled and sliced

Salt and pepper, to taste

STEPS

1 Toast the bread slices. Top with smoked
   salmon, avocado, and strawberries.
   Season, and serve.

VINAIGRETTE BAR

BEST BEFORE

Keeps for a few months in the fridge.

CATEGORIES

Gift · Economical · Quick & easy · Lactose free · Gluten free · Vegetarian

QUANTITY : *¾ to 1 cup* · 5 MIN · *Doesn't freeze well.*

I'm not the type to disparage store-bought products; in fact, I'm the first to jump at a jar of grocery store jam or chicken broth whenever I'm in a rush. I love to cook and feed myself well, but not at the expense of my sanity (as my mother would say); therefore, I've got to be realistic about available time to prepare a meal.

That said, there's one thing I categorically refuse to buy at the grocery store and I never compromise on: my homemade vinaigrette. Making a good vinaigrette from basic ingredients you probably already have on hand is so quick and simple, and tastes so much better.

Whether for a green salad, quinoa, or pasta, or simply to drizzle over vegetables fresh from the garden, served with cheese, vinaigrettes are at the heart of our menu. As such, I suggest four recipes that can be prepared in one step and using only a few ingredients.

CONTINUED ON PAGE 110

CONTINUED FROM PAGE 109

PONZU VINAIGRETTE

INGREDIENTS

¼ cup olive oil

¼ cup vegetable oil

¼ cup lemon juice

2 tbsp soy sauce (or tamari)

2 tsp honey

Black pepper, to taste

RASPBERRY & BALSAMIC VINAIGRETTE

INGREDIENTS

¼ cup canola oil

¼ cup olive oil

1 tbsp raspberry jam

2 tbsp balsamic vinegar

1 tbsp Dijon mustard

Salt and pepper, to taste

ORANGE & POPPY SEED VINAIGRETTE

INGREDIENTS

¼ cup orange juice

¼ cup olive oil

2 tbsp ketchup

2 tbsp sherry vinegar

1 clove garlic, chopped

2 tsp poppy seeds

CREAMY TARRAGON VINAIGRETTE

INGREDIENTS

½ cup mayonnaise

¼ cup water

1 tbsp apple cider vinegar

1 tbsp grainy mustard

1 tsp maple syrup

2 tbsp chopped fresh tarragon

STEPS

1   In a bowl, whisk together all the ingredients of the chosen vinaigrette. Season to taste.

CRUNCHY VEGETABLE SALAD
WITH FETA DRESSING

QUANTITY : *6 servings* · 20 MIN · *Doesn't freeze well.*

I was sick for the first twenty weeks of my pregnancy, and the only things I could eat were Tim Horton's bagels and cream cheese, feta, and small and crunchy foods.

After the nausea passed, I entered a phase where I craved candy made with artificial flavours. Late at night, I would ask Alex to go buy me sour gums, just to devour the entire bag, exclaiming the whole time how impressed I was that they could artificially recreate real fruit flavour — truly dignified behaviour for a cookbook author.

All this to say that my questionable tastes forced me to develop recipes that will go down in history as household classics, like this lovely and delicious crunchy salad, which is perfect. It's so simple that I'd never thought of it before. Raw vegetables, served with dip, made all the better chopped into small pieces and tossed in a feta cheese dressing. Try it yourself, alongside a bit of grilled fish or meat.

BEST BEFORE

Keeps for 2 to 3 days in the fridge.

CATEGORIES

*Economical · Entertaining · Gluten free
Vegetarian*

STEPS

1   In a bowl, combine all the salad ingredients.

2   In another bowl, whisk together all the dressing ingredients. Pour over the salad, toss to combine, and adjust the seasoning to taste.

INGREDIENTS

FOR THE SALAD

1 cup thinly sliced green beans

1 cup finely diced celery

1 cup chopped baby carrots (cut into rounds)

1 small bulb fennel, finely diced

1 red bell pepper, finely diced

6 radishes, finely diced

2 green onions, finely sliced

Salt and pepper, to taste

FOR THE DRESSING

½ cup crumbled feta cheese

¼ cup lemon juice

¼ cup chopped fresh basil

1 tbsp chopped fresh oregano

⅓ cup vegetable oil

Salt and pepper, to taste

TIP

If you've got good-quality olive oil on hand, substitute it for the vegetable oil.

The colour of this mix gives the illusion that the keftas are made with ground beef, making this the perfect recipe to try to trick carnivorous friends who claim not to like vegetarian recipes (diabolical laughter).

BEET KEFTAS WITH SPICY YOGURT SAUCE & HUMMUS

114

BEST BEFORE - *Keeps for 1 week in the fridge.*

CATEGORIES - *Economical · Entertaining · Vegetarian*

INGREDIENTS

1 can (19 oz) pinto beans, rinsed and drained

2 medium beets, cooked, peeled, and quartered

½ cup sunflower seeds

½ cup walnuts

2 tbsp grainy mustard

2 cloves garlic

½ cup chopped fresh basil

2 tsp baking powder

1 tsp ground cumin

1 tsp ground coriander

½ cup all-purpose flour

Salt and pepper, to taste

Vegetable oil, for cooking

FOR THE SAUCE

½ cup store-bought or homemade hummus

⅓ cup sour cream (or plain yogurt)

1 tbsp Sriracha sauce

STEPS

1 In a bowl, combine all the sauce ingredients. Set aside.

2 In a food processor, combine the pinto beans, beets, sunflower seeds, walnuts, mustard, garlic, and basil, and process until smooth. Transfer to a large bowl.

3 Add the baking powder, cumin, coriander, and flour. Season generously, and stir well. Set aside.

4 Fill a non-stick pan with 1 cm of vegetable oil, and heat over medium heat. Using a spoon, form egg-size balls of the bean mixture into croquettes. Working in batches, gently place them in the oil and cook for about 2 to 3 minutes on each side, or until nicely browned.

5 Drain the cooked croquettes on paper towel. Serve with the sauce.

SOBA NOODLE & VEGETABLE SALAD WITH PEANUT SAUCE

BEST BEFORE - *Keeps for 3 to 4 days in the fridge.*

CATEGORIES - *Quick & easy · Lactose free · Gluten free*

117

INGREDIENTS

2 servings soba noodles

1 tbsp olive oil

*1 cup broccoli florets, cut into pieces
    (or rapini)*

1 cup snow peas, trimmed

Juice of 1 lime

1 cup julienned or grated zucchini

1 cup julienned or grated carrots

1 cup bean sprouts

Salt and pepper, to taste

*¼ cup roasted peanuts, chopped,
    for garnish*

FOR THE SAUCE

¼ cup peanut butter

2 tbsp olive oil (or vegetable oil)

3 tbsp rice vinegar

1 tsp sesame oil

2 tbsp honey

Salt and pepper, to taste

STEPS

1 In a bowl, whisk together the peanut butter and olive oil. Add the remaining sauce ingredients, and whisk well. Set aside.

2 Bring a pot of water to a boil. Cook the soba noodles according to the package directions. Drain and let cool.

3 In a pan, over medium heat, heat the olive oil. Sauté the broccoli and snow peas for 5 minutes. Drizzle with the lime juice, and transfer to a salad bowl.

4 Add the remaining ingredients, as well as the sauce, and stir well. Serve with the chopped peanuts.

CHIPOTLE CHICKEN & PURÉED AVOCADO SANDWICH

BEST BEFORE - *Serve immediately or the next day.*

CATÉGORIE - *Indulgent*

INGREDIENTS

FOR THE CHICKEN

2 boneless, skinless chicken breasts, cut into strips

1 tbsp vegetable oil

Zest and juice of 1 lime

1 tsp steak spice

1 chipotle pepper in adobo sauce, chopped

½ cup sour cream

FOR THE SANDWICH

2 ciabatta buns

4 artichoke hearts, finely chopped

4 slices Swiss cheese (or cheese of your choice)

1 ripe avocado

Juice of ½ lime

Salt and pepper, to taste

STEPS

1   Preheat the oven to 400°F, with the rack in centre position. Line a baking sheet with parchment paper. Set aside.

2   In a pan, over medium heat, heat the oil. Add the chicken strips, and sauté until cooked through and nicely browned. Stir in the remaining chicken ingredients and continue cooking for 1 minute. Set aside.

3   Cut the buns in half and place them on the baking sheet. Top with the chicken mixture, the artichokes, and the cheese.

4   Bake for 15 minutes.

5   Meanwhile, in a bowl, combine the avocado and lime juice. Mash together using a fork. Season. Serve on the side, with the sandwich.

TIP

The chicken mixture is so good, it deserves to be served on its own, in tacos, on rice, or with anything else your heart desires.

CHICKEN COLESLAW WITH
CREAMY LEMONGRASS DRESSING

QUANTITY : *6 servings*   ·   🥄 *20 MIN*   ·   *Doesn't freeze well.*

BEST BEFORE   -   *Keeps for 2 to 3 days in the fridge.*

CATEGORIES   -   *Economical · Entertaining · Lactose free*

INGREDIENTS

FOR THE COLESLAW

4 cups thinly sliced Chinese cabbage

2 cups julienned or grated carrots

2 cups julienned or grated daikon (white radish)

2 green onions, minced

1 ½ cups finely diced cooked chicken

FOR THE DRESSING

⅓ cup mayonnaise

3 tbsp grated lemongrass

2 tbsp rice vinegar

1 tsp fish sauce

1 tsp Sriracha sauce

1 tsp sugar

Salt and pepper, to taste

STEPS

1   In a large salad bowl, combine all the coleslaw ingredients. Set aside.

2   In a small bowl, whisk together all the dressing ingredients.

3   Pour the dressing over the coleslaw. Toss well, and serve.

TIP

Lemongrass sticks can be found in the specialty herbs section of most grocery stores and will keep for a long time in the fridge or freezer. The best way to prepare lemongrass is to grate it with a zester. For a very fragrant condiment, grate a large quantity of it into oil.

HIS
CHOICE

YELLOW BEET SALAD WITH BLOOD ORANGES & LENTILS

BEST BEFORE - *Keeps for 3 to 4 days in the fridge.*

CATEGORIES - *Economical · Lactose free · Gluten free · Vegetarian*

INGREDIENTS

5 to 6 medium yellow beets

½ cup Puy lentils (see tip below)

Salt and pepper, to taste

½ cup walnuts, roughly chopped

1 cup packed kale leaves, thinly sliced

2 blood oranges, peeled and pith removed, sliced into thin rounds

½ cup sprouts of your choice (radish, arugula, red cabbage, etc.)

FOR THE VINAIGRETTE

¼ cup olive oil

3 tbsp white balsamic vinegar

2 tbsp honey

1 tbsp Dijon mustard

Salt and pepper, to taste

STEPS

1   In a bowl, combine all the vinaigrette ingredients. Set aside.

2   Put the beets (with the skins on) in a pot and cover with water. Cover the pot with the lid and bring to a boil. Reduce the heat and simmer for 40 minutes to 1 hour (depending on the beet size), until tender. Drain, and let the beets cool for at least 1 hour in the fridge.

3   Bring a pot of water to a boil. Add the lentils, and cook for 20 minutes, or until tender. Drain and set aside to cool.

4   Peel the beets, halve them, and cut them into thin slices. Transfer to a large salad bowl, and season. Add the vinaigrette, along with the remaining ingredients, and stir well. Adjust the seasoning to taste. Serve.

LUNCH & SALADS

TIP

If you don't like lentils, you can substitute with and equal amount of quinoa, couscous, barley, orzo, etc.

Do you have cucumbers, tomatoes, mint, parsley, and thyme in your garden?
It's time to take advantage of them with this intentionally simple recipe. Biting into freshly picked vegetables is an amazing gastronomical experience, so I didn't want to bury their taste under a mountain of overwhelming flavours.

This recipe might seem a bit bland at first, and to tell you the truth, I wasn't sure whether to include it in the book. However, I ultimately decided there were likely others who were just as in love with their gardens as I am, and they'd be happy for a simple, easy-to-make recipe to enjoy their harvest. As for the rest of you, I hope I've piqued your curiosity and made you want to start a little garden of your own next summer.

BEST BEFORE - *Keeps for 2 to 3 days in the fridge.*

CATEGORIES - *Economical · Quick & easy · Gluten free · Vegetarian*

INGREDIENTS

1 cup labneh (Lebanese fresh cheese), for serving

FOR THE SALAD

1 can (19 oz) mixed beans, rinsed and drained

2 cups cherry tomatoes, halved

2 cups halved and sliced cucumber

½ cup minced red onion

¼ cup chopped fresh mint

½ cup roughly chopped fresh parsley

½ cup Kalamata olives, pitted

Salt and pepper, to taste

FOR THE VINAIGRETTE

⅓ cup olive oil (or light-tasting oil)

1 clove garlic, chopped

2 tbsp sherry vinegar

Juice of ½ lemon

1 tsp chopped fresh thyme leaves

2 tbsp toasted sesame seeds

½ tsp salt

STEPS

1 In a large salad bowl, combine all the salad ingredients. Set aside.

2 In a small bowl, whisk together all the vinaigrette ingredients. Pour over the salad.

3 Toss, adjust the seasoning to taste, and serve.

BEAN SALAD WITH
OLIVES & LABNEH

QUANTITY : *4–6 servings* · 15 MIN · *Doesn't freeze well.*

CHAPTER

No. 4

—

SOUPS

STRACCIATELLA
(ITALIAN EGG SOUP)

Stracciatella, a word I like to pronounce firmly and using a strong accent, is an Italian specialty in which beaten eggs are added to hot chicken broth. In seconds, the egg transforms into delicious strands. It's like eating scrambled eggs in a heavenly broth.

I personally like to add a little homemade tomato sauce to the middle of each bowl to give some colour to the dish, but that's optional.

BEST BEFORE - *Keeps for 2 to 3 days in the fridge.*

CATEGORIES - *Economical · Entertaining · Quick & easy*

SOUPS

INGREDIENTS

*4 cups chicken broth, store-bought or homemade
(see recipe on page 155)*

2 green onions, minced

1 clove garlic, finely chopped

⅓ cup soup pasta, or to taste

2 cups baby spinach

Salt and pepper, to taste

2 eggs

¼ cup freshly grated Parmesan cheese

*½ cup homemade tomato sauce (or canned
crushed tomatoes)*

STEPS

1 In a large pot, combine the chicken broth, green onions, and garlic and bring to a boil. Add the pasta, cover the pot with the lid, and cook according to pasta package directions.

2 Stir in the spinach, and continue cooking for 1 minute. Season generously.

3 In a bowl, whisk together the eggs and Parmesan. Season. Add the egg mixture to the soup. Using a whisk, stir once, and then cook without stirring for 30 seconds.

4 Adjust the seasoning to taste. Serve with a little tomato sauce in the middle of each bowl.

QUANTITY : *4 servings* · 🥄 5 MIN · 🕐 10 MIN · *Doesn't freeze well.*

CREAMY YELLOW BEET & CORN SOUP

BEST BEFORE - *Keeps for 1 week in the fridge.*

CATEGORIES - *Economical · Gluten free*

INGREDIENTS

2 tbsp butter

1 yellow onion, minced

Salt and pepper, to taste

2 cups yellow beets, peeled and sliced

1 cup corn kernels (fresh or frozen)

2 tbsp maple syrup

4 cups chicken broth

¼ cup chopped fresh dill

½ cup sour cream

STEPS

1 In a pot, over medium heat, melt the butter. Add the onion, and cook for 5 minutes, or until softened. Season.

2 Add the beets, corn, and maple syrup. Season again, and continue cooking for 2 to 3 minutes.

3 Add the broth, and bring to a boil. Reduce the heat and simmer gently for 30 minutes.

4 Remove the pot from the heat. Stir in the dill and sour cream. Transfer the mixture to a food processor and process until smooth and creamy. Adjust the seasoning to taste. Serve.

CREAM OF CHICKPEA, CURRY & BACON SOUP

BEST BEFORE - *Keeps for 1 week in the fridge.*

CATEGORIES - *Economical · Indulgent · Quick & easy · Gluten free*

INGREDIENTS

1 tbsp butter

4 strips bacon, thinly sliced

1 yellow onion, minced

1 tbsp curry powder

2 cans (19 oz each) chickpeas, rinsed and drained

4 cups beef broth

Salt and pepper, to taste

½ cup 15% cream

STEPS

1   In a large pot, over medium heat, melt the butter. Add the bacon and onion, and cook for 5 minutes, or until the bacon is cooked through and the onion is browned.

2   Stir in the curry powder, chickpeas, and broth. Season generously, and bring to a boil.

3   Reduce the heat to low, cover the pot with the lid, and simmer for 15 minutes.

4   Stir in the cream. Transfer the mixture to a food processor, and process until smooth. Adjust the seasoning to taste. Serve.

QUANTITY : *8 servings* · 🥄 30 MIN · 🕐 40 MIN · *Freezes well.*

GREEN VEGGIE MINESTRONE WITH HERB GARNISH

INGREDIENTS

FOR THE SOUP

1 cup dried green lentils

1 tbsp butter

4 green onions, minced

2 cloves garlic, chopped

1 medium fennel bulb, finely diced

Salt and pepper, to taste

8 cups vegetable broth

Zest and juice of 1 lemon

1 cup chopped (½ inch) green beans

2 zucchini, cut into 1 cm dice

1 cup frozen sweet peas

1 tbsp chopped fresh oregano

FOR THE HERB GARNISH

½ cup fresh basil

7 to 8 fresh mint leaves

Zest and juice of ½ lemon

⅓ cup olive oil

Salt and pepper, to taste

BEST BEFORE
Keeps for about 1 week in the fridge.

CATEGORIES
Lactose free · Gluten free · Vegetarian

135

STEPS

1   Rinse the lentils well, and set aside.

2   In a large pot, over medium heat, melt the butter. Add the green onions, garlic, and fennel, and sauté for 5 minutes. Season.

3   Stir in the lentils and broth, season again, and bring to a boil.

4   Reduce the heat, cover the pot with the lid, and simmer for 30 minutes.

5   Add the remaining soup ingredients, and continue cooking, uncovered, for 5 minutes. Adjust the seasoning, to taste.

6   Combine all the herb garnish ingredients in a food processor, and process until smooth. Serve on top of the soup.

SOUPS

TIP

The herb garnish makes the dish look pretty, but you can also stir it directly into the cooked soup.

You know a soup is good when, upon eating it in Mexico, your face turns deep red, your body runs out of sweat, and you'd be willing to sell your husband to finance research on a personal air conditioner.

That was the inspiration for this fantastic recipe, which has since become one of Alex's favourites, so much so that he can't stop talking about it. (Obviously, I'd never really sell him!)

TORTILLA SOUP

BEST BEFORE - *Keeps for 1 week in the fridge.*

CATEGORIES - *Economical · Quick & easy · Gluten free*

INGREDIENTS

FOR THE SOUP

1 tbsp olive oil

1 yellow onion, minced

1 clove garlic, minced

1 red bell pepper, seeded and cut into strips

1 jalapeño pepper, seeded and minced

1 tsp ground cumin

1 can (28 oz) whole tomatoes

4 cups chicken broth

1 ½ cups plain tortilla corn chips, crumbled

Juice of 1 lime

Salt and pepper, to taste

FOR THE TOPPING

½ cup shredded cheddar cheese

Tortilla corn chips, for serving (optional)

STEPS

1 In a large pot, over medium heat, heat the olive oil. Add the onion, garlic, and red and jalapeño peppers, and cook for 5 minutes, or until softened.

2 Add the remaining soup ingredients, and bring to a boil.

3 Reduce the heat, cover the pot with the lid, and simmer for 15 minutes.

4 Using an immersion or regular blender, blend the soup until smooth and creamy. Serve with the cheddar cheese and tortilla chips.

HIS
CHOICE

BLACK BEAN SOUP

BEST BEFORE
Keeps for 1 week in the fridge.

CATEGORIES
Economical · Quick & easy · Lactose free · Gluten free · Vegetarian

INGREDIENTS

*1 can (19 oz) black beans, rinsed
  and drained*

1 can (28 oz) diced tomatoes

1 tbsp olive oil

1 red bell pepper, seeded and finely diced

1 yellow onion, chopped

2 cloves garlic, chopped

Salt and pepper, to taste

2 cups water

1 cup corn kernels (fresh or frozen)

2 tsp ground cumin

1 tsp ground coriander

1 tsp sweet paprika

Zest and juice of 1 lime

2 tbsp maple syrup

STEPS

1   In a food processor, combine 1 cup of the black beans and 1 cup of the diced tomatoes, and process until smooth. Set aside.

2   In a large pot, over medium heat, heat the olive oil. Add the red pepper, onion, and garlic, and sauté for 5 minutes. Season.

3   Add the remaining ingredients, along with the blended mixture from Step 1 and the remaining black beans and tomatoes.

4   Bring to a boil, cover the pot with the lid, and reduce the heat to low. Simmer for 15 minutes. Adjust the seasoning to taste. Serve.

SOUPS

COLD AVOCADO, MANGO & CUCUMBER SOUP WITH NORDIC SHRIMP

I don't know if there are any Columbos out there, but anyone observant will notice that in the photo I blended the oil and cilantro for the topping before mixing them with the shrimp. Honestly, this step isn't really necessary; it just means more dishes to wash. The final result will be just as good.

INGREDIENTS

FOR THE SOUP

2 avocados, stoned and peeled

1 Ataulfo mango, peeled and pitted

1 English cucumber, peeled

Juice of ½ lime

2 tbsp fresh cilantro

1 tsp sambal oelek

1 ½ cups water

Salt and pepper, to taste

FOR THE TOPPING

2 tbsp olive oil

¼ cup chopped fresh cilantro

¾ cup Nordic shrimp

Salt and pepper, to taste

BEST BEFORE

Keeps for 2 to 3 days in the fridge.

CATEGORIES

Quick & easy · Lactose free · Gluten free

STEPS

1 In a food processor, combine all the soup ingredients, and process until smooth and creamy. Cover and refrigerate until chilled.

2 In a bowl, combine all the topping ingredients. Serve with the well-chilled soup.

TIP

This soup is also delicious without the shrimp topping.

LEEK, CELERY & LETTUCE SOUP WITH EXPRESS GOAT CHEESE GNOCCHI

QUANTITY : *4 servings* · 🥄 20 MIN · 🕐 40 MIN · *Freezes well.*

I confess that I'm pretty creative when it comes to cooking whatever's leftover in the fridge, but I'd be lying if I said I get inspired by old, wilting lettuce. That's why the salad lover in me is so happy to have this soup to fall back on, to avoid wasting leftover lettuce.

Not only that, but these express goat cheese gnocchi are insanely good. They are easy to prepare in advance and, believe me, are the type of side dish that pairs perfectly with many of your favourite soups and salads.

CONTINUED ON PAGE 145

CONTINUED FROM PAGE 142

BEST BEFORE - *Keeps for 1 week in the fridge.*

CATEGORIES - *Economical · Vegetarian*

INGREDIENTS

FOR THE SOUP

1 tbsp butter

1 medium leek, finely chopped

2 cups finely chopped celery

Salt and pepper, to taste

*1 cup peeled and finely chopped
    yellow potatoes*

4 cups chicken broth (or vegetable broth)

*2 cups finely chopped lettuce (curly,
    romaine, mesclun, watercress, spinach,
    arugula, etc.)*

FOR THE GNOCCHI

½ cup (3 ½ oz) goat cheese

¼ cup all-purpose flour

2 tbsp chopped fresh parsley

STEPS

FOR THE SOUP

1 In a pot, over medium heat, melt the butter. Add the leek and celery, and sauté for 5 minutes. Season generously.

2 Stir in the potatoes and chicken broth. Bring to a boil, cover the pot with the lid, and reduce the heat to low. Simmer for 20 minutes.

3 Add the lettuce, and continue cooking for 2 minutes. Season again.

4 Using an immersion or regular blender, blend the soup until smooth and creamy. Adjust the seasoning to taste.

FOR THE GNOCCHI

5 Preheat the oven to 400°F. Line a baking sheet with parchment paper, and set aside.

6 In a bowl, using a fork, mix together all the gnocchi ingredients.

7 On a floured work surface, roll the dough into a long log about ¾ inches in diameter.

8 Cut gnocchi in ½-inch lengths, and arrange them in a single layer on the baking sheet. Bake for 15 minutes. Serve in the soup.

What follows is one of my favourite recipes from this chapter. I know it's not a classic miso soup recipe, but that's for a good reason: I wanted to make it from ingredients that are easy to find at the grocery store.

That said, if you have the chance, I highly recommend that you take a trip down to your local Asian grocery store. They're really cool, and I know we don't take the time to go often enough.

BEST BEFORE - *Keeps for 1 week in the fridge.*

CATEGORIES - *Lactose free · Gluten free*

INGREDIENTS

FOR THE BROTH

¼ cup miso paste

½ cup water

3 green onions, finely sliced

2 sheets nori (sushi seaweed)

2 tsp fish sauce

2 tbsp soy sauce (or tamari)

6 cups water

FOR THE GARNISH

2 green onions, finely sliced

1 package (1 lb) soft tofu, cut into ½-inch cubes

4 servings soba noodles

2 cups mini bok choy, quartered

STEPS

1 In a bowl, whisk together the miso and ½ cup water. Set aside.

2 In a large pot, combine the green onions, nori, fish sauce, soy sauce, and water. Bring to a boil, cover the pot with the lid, and reduce the heat to low. Simmer for 20 minutes, or until the nori begins to dissolve.

3 Add the garnish ingredients, and continue to simmer for 8 minutes.

4 Add the miso mixture, and stir well. Adjust the seasoning to taste. Serve.

MISO SOUP WITH TOFU
& SOBA NOODLES

QUANTITY : *4 servings* · 🥄 10 MIN · 🕐 25 MIN · *Doesn't freeze well.*

QUANTITY : *4 servings* · 🥄 30 MIN · 🕐 30 MIN · *Freezes well (see tip on page 150).*

HOMEMADE WONTON SOUP

CONTINUED FROM PAGE 149

STEP 1

Put the stuffing in the centre of the wonton wrapper. Brush the four sides with egg white.

150

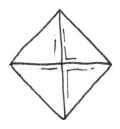

STEP 2

Fold the outer edges toward the centre to form a diamond.

SOUPS

STEP 3

Press the sides together to seal the stuffing in the wrapper.

TIP

The broth and uncooked wontons freeze well, but separately. Also, I strongly suggest only cooking the amount of wontons you're planning to eat because they don't stay together well in the broth.

The broth keeps for about 2 weeks in the fridge, without the wontons.

CATEGORIES

Entertaining · Lactose free

INGREDIENTS

20 store-bought wonton wrappers

1 egg white, beaten

Green onions, finely sliced (for garnish)

Crispy noodles (for garnish)

FOR THE BROTH

Dash of vegetable oil

4 green onions, finely sliced

1 tbsp chopped peeled fresh ginger

2 cloves garlic, chopped

3 stalks celery, finely sliced

6 cups chicken broth

2 tsp rice vinegar

1 tbsp soy sauce

FOR THE STUFFING

½ lb ground pork

1 tbsp chopped peeled fresh ginger

1 green onion, chopped

2 tbsp soy sauce

½ tsp fish sauce

½ tsp baking soda

STEPS

1   In a large pot, over medium heat, heat the vegetable oil. Add the green onions, ginger, garlic, and celery, and sauté for 5 minutes. Stir in the remaining broth ingredients and bring to a boil.

2   Reduce the heat and simmer gently for 15 minutes. Set aside.

3   In a bowl, combine all the stuffing ingredients.

4   Lay out a few wonton wrappers on a work surface. Top each with 1 tsp of stuffing. Brush the sides with the egg white. Gather the four corners and press the sides in to form small square dumplings. (See the diagram on page 150.)

5   Bring the broth back to a boil, and add the desired number of wontons (calculate 4 to 5 per person). Simmer for 6 minutes for fresh dumplings or 8 minutes for frozen.

6   Garnish with green onions and crispy noodles. Serve.

149

SOUPS

CONTINUED ON PAGE 150

HIS CHOICE

QUANTITY : *3 litres* · 🥢 5 MIN · 🕐 2 H · *Freezes well.*

HOMEMADE BROTHS

CATEGORIES
Economical · Lactose free · Gluten free · Vegetarian

I'll be the first to admit to buying prepared chicken and vegetable broth when I'm in a bind. After all, store-bought broth isn't too bad, and using it definitely seems to save a lot more time and energy than if we'd made it ourselves, right? Not true.

Making your own broth isn't only tastier and healthier, but it's also a good way to give many foods a second life, and save money too.

I recommend filling up freezer bags, slowly but surely, every day, whenever you cook, with the trimmings from your veggies, fresh herbs, meat bones, etc. That way, leftover vegetable and onion peels, as well as meat trimmings and cartilage, that otherwise would've been thrown out will be the stars of your next batch of broth. It doesn't cost anything, and it does wonders for your conscience.

That said, avoid adding things with really strong flavours (ginger, cilantro, mint, tarragon, etc.) to your broths, and instead save them for recipes where the flavours won't clash.

CONTINUED ON PAGE 154

CONTINUED FROM PAGE 153

Straining and skimming

To skim the fat from my broth (after straining it, of course), I used to let it cool completely in the fridge until a solid layer of fat formed on top. Then I'd remove it using a spoon. However, I recently learned a lightning-fast trick that strains and skims at the same time. Simply put a layer of paper towel in the bottom of a sieve and pour the broth through it. The paper towel traps all the solids and a good portion of the fat. Magic!

Freezing

I recommend freezing portions of broth in freezer bags that hold 2 to 4 cups, and writing the type of broth on the bag. Whenever I do it, I pour the broth into ice-cube trays to make bouillon cubes; once frozen I transfer the cubes to a freezer bag. They come in really handy when you're improvising a weeknight meal, and a little homemade broth is just the thing to take a whole recipe up a notch.

CHICKEN BROTH

INGREDIENTS

1 chicken carcass (or about 4 cups chicken bones)

1 yellow onion, roughly chopped

2 carrots, cut lengthwise

1 clove garlic, crushed

½ cup chopped fresh parsley (stems or leaves)

1 bay leaf

1 tsp whole black peppercorns

12 cups water

VEGETABLE BROTH

INGREDIENTS

2 yellow onions, roughly chopped

2 carrots, cut lengthwise

2 stalks celery, finely sliced

2 cloves garlic, crushed

1 tomato, diced (or 1 tbsp tomato paste)

2 sprigs oregano (or dried oregano)

½ cup chopped fresh parsley (stems or leaves)

1 bay leaf

1 tsp whole black peppercorns

12 cups water

STEPS

IN A LARGE POT

1   Combine all the ingredients. Bring to a boil, reduce the heat, and simmer, uncovered, for 2 hours.

2   Let cool, then strain. Salt to taste.

IN A SLOW COOKER

1   Place all the ingredients in a slow cooker, cover with the lid, and cook on low for 8 to 10 hours.

2   Let cool, then strain. Salt to taste.

CHAPTER

No.⁵

—

FISH &
SEAFOOD

COD WITH
POTATO SOUP
& FRESH CORN

159

QUANTITY : *4 servings* · 🥄 20 MIN · 🕐 30 MIN · *Doesn't freeze well.*

BEST BEFORE - *Serve immediately.*

CATEGORIES - *Entertaining · Lactose free · Gluten free*

Alex and I were on St. Denis Street, in Montreal, in a little restaurant we love when I ordered the original version of this recipe. Two years have passed since then, but I remember it like it was yesterday — that's how much I enjoyed the dish. I also remember saying to Alex, at least 100 times, what a good idea it was to serve fish over soup. In response, he's asked me 50 times to go back to that restaurant, which hasn't happened yet. So I decided to try to recreate the dish for this book, to satisfy my taste buds and my memories.

To end with a little anecdote: I also remember how we stuffed our faces with dessert later that night (a little nostalgia, thinking back to the days before Alex was diabetic). As we were leaving the restaurant, we decided, on a whim, to go to the La Ronde amusement park. We thought we were so cool, being spontaneous just like in the movies, until we got off the Goliath with green complexions. We decided to boost our morales with beaver tails, to put the icing on the cake of bad decisions.

CONTINUED ON PAGE 160

CONTINUED FROM PAGE 159

INGREDIENTS

FOR THE SOUP

1 tbsp butter

½ yellow onion, chopped

1 cup corn kernels (fresh or frozen)

1 cup peeled and cubed yellow potatoes

1 ½ cups chicken broth

2 tsp balsamic vinegar

1 tsp vanilla extract

Salt and pepper, to taste

FOR THE FISH

Salt and pepper, to taste

4 cod loins (4 ½ oz each), skinless (see tips below)

1 tbsp olive oil

1 tbsp butter

FOR THE SALAD

2 cups arugula

½ cup corn kernels (fresh or frozen), cooked

1 tbsp balsamic vinegar

1 tbsp olive oil

TIP

Cod loin is the thickest part of a cod fillet and has in recent years become more readily available, making for nice, juicy portions that cook evenly.

You can also use another white fish of your choice: halibut, haddock, flounder, walleye, etc.

FOR THE SOUP

1   In a pot, over medium heat, melt the butter. Add the onion, and sauté for 3 minutes, or until tender. Add the remaining soup ingredients, and bring to a boil. Reduce the heat to low and simmer, uncovered, for 15 minutes.

2   In a food processor, process the soup until smooth. You can pass the mixture through a fine-mesh sieve to obtain a perfect texture, but it's not necessary. Adjust the seasoning to taste, and set aside, keeping warm.

FOR THE FISH

3   Season the fish fillets.

4   In a non-stick pan, over high heat, heat the olive oil. Add the butter and fish. Don't disturb the fish until it's nicely golden brown (about 4 minutes). Reduce the heat to medium, flip the fish, and continue cooking for 3 to 4 minutes.

FOR THE SALAD

5   Meanwhile, in a salad bowl, combine all the salad ingredients.

ASSEMBLY

6   To serve, spoon a big ladleful of soup into a bowl. Top with a fish fillet and some salad.

Horseradish is readily available at most grocery stores. It's usually located in the condiments section with a label on the jar that reads "prepared horseradish." You can use it to make horseradish whipped cream for your fish dishes, or add it to mashed potatoes, vinaigrettes, etc.

QUANTITY : *12 croquettes or 4 servings* · 🥄 20 MIN · 🕐 8 MIN · *Freezes well.*

SALMON & TOFU CROQUETTES WITH PICKLE SAUCE

INGREDIENTS

FOR THE CROQUETTES

1 cup cooked salmon or 1 can (7 ½ oz) salmon

9 oz firm tofu

3 green onions, finely sliced

¼ cup chopped fresh dill

½ cup all-purpose flour

2 tsp baking powder

3 tbsp ketchup

2 tsp store-bought horseradish (see tip below)

Juice of 1 lemon

Salt and pepper, to taste

2 tbsp vegetable oil, for cooking

FOR THE SAUCE

1 ripe avocado

½ cup chopped garlic pickles

2 tbsp chopped fresh dill

¼ cup water

Juice of ¼ lemon

BEST BEFORE
Keeps for 2 to 3 days in the fridge.

CATEGORIES
Economical · Quick & easy · Lactose free

STEPS

1   In a food processor, combine all the sauce ingredients, and process until smooth. Set aside.

2   In the food processor, combine the salmon, tofu, green onions, and dill and process until well incorporated. Transfer to a large bowl, and add the remaining croquette ingredients. Season generously. Using your hands, form 12 patties (about ¼ cup each). Set aside.

3   In a large non-stick pan, over medium heat, heat the oil. Cook the patties for about 3 to 4 minutes per side, or until golden brown. Serve with the sauce.

QUANTITY : *2 servings* · 🥄 10 MIN · 🕐 15 MIN · *Doesn't freeze well.*

MUSSELS IN CREAMY PANCETTA & LEEK SAUCE

INGREDIENTS

1 tbsp butter

4 slices pancetta, chopped

1 medium leek, finely sliced

2 stalks celery, finely sliced

1 cup diced (½ inch) Yukon Gold potatoes

¼ cup dry white wine

1 tbsp grainy mustard

⅓ cup 35% cream

1 bag (2 lbs) fresh mussels

STEPS

1 In a big pot with a lid, over medium-high heat, melt the butter. Add the pancetta, leek, celery, and potatoes, and sauté for 8 minutes.

2 Add the white wine, mustard, and cream, and cook, stirring, for 2 minutes.

3 Add the mussels, stir, and cover the pot with the lid. Bring to a boil. Continue cooking for 3 to 4 minutes, using a large spoon to stir the mussels a few times (this will help them open). Once all the mussels are open, the meal is ready. (Discard any mussels that do not open.)

STORING THE FRESH MUSSELS

Mussels are alive when we buy them so they have to remain well-ventilated until cooked. Therefore, store them in a well-ventilated bowl in the fridge, or cover with plastic wrap with holes cut into it. Avoid putting mussels in a sealed container.

SORTING THE FRESH MUSSELS

First, rinse them well, and remove any with broken shells. For any that are slightly opened, bang the base of the shell on a hard surface. If they begin to slowly close up, keep them. If not, discard them.

CLEANING THE LEEK

Leeks often have dirt trapped inside them. The best trick for cleaning them is to slice them first, then place them in a sieve and rinse them well. That way, the dirt is easily removed.

THE SAUCE

The sauce will be thick and seem insufficient before you add the mussels to the pot. While cooking, the mussels release a lot of liquid — enough to easily double the amount of sauce.

165

FISH & SEAFOOD

I find it funny when people say they don't like the taste of snails, because, honestly, they don't taste like much. I was very pleased to come up with three completely different sauces to give maximum flavour to a meal that's too often overlooked.

There are a couple of ways to serve snails: in little individual ramekins with fresh bread, on a big serving platter for sharing, over toasted bread, or on Portobello mushrooms baked in the oven.

CLASSIC GARLIC SNAILS

QUANTITY : *4 servings* · 🥄 8 MIN · 🕐 6 MIN · *Freezes well.*

BEST BEFORE - *Keeps for 2 to 3 days in the fridge.*

CATEGORIES - *Economical · Indulgent · Entertaining · Quick & easy · Lactose free · Gluten free*

INGREDIENTS

1 tbsp butter

1 shallot, chopped

2 cloves garlic, chopped

1 can (4 ½ oz) snails, rinsed and drained

Salt and pepper, to taste

½ cup butter, cubed

Juice of ½ lemon

2 tbsp chopped fresh parsley

STEPS

1   In a pan, over medium heat, melt the butter. Add the shallot and garlic, and sauté for 2 minutes. Add the snails, and continue cooking for 1 minute. Season.

2   Add the remaining ingredients, reduce the heat to low, and cook for 2 to 3 minutes. Adjust the seasoning to taste. Serve.

CONTINUED ON PAGE 168

CONTINUED FROM PAGE 166

SNAILS WITH BLUE CHEESE & WHITE WINE

QUANTITY : *4 servings* · *6 MIN* · *8 MIN* · *Doesn't freeze well.*

BEST BEFORE - *Keeps for 2 to 3 days in the fridge.*

CATEGORIES - *Indulgent · Entertaining · Quick & easy · Gluten free*

INGREDIENTS

1 tbsp butter

1 shallot, chopped

2 cloves garlic, chopped

1 can (4 ½ oz) snails, rinsed and drained

Salt and pepper, to taste

¼ cup dry white wine

½ cup 35% cream

2 tbsp crumbled blue cheese

STEPS

1   In a pan, over medium heat, melt the butter. Add the shallot and garlic, and sauté for 2 minutes. Add the snails, and continue cooking for 1 minute. Season.

2   Add the remaining ingredients, reduce the heat to low, and cook for 5 minutes. Adjust the seasoning to taste. Serve.

SNAILS WITH CHORIZO
& MOZZARELLA

QUANTITY : *4 servings* · 🥄 10 MIN · 🕐 8 MIN · *Doesn't freeze well.*

BEST BEFORE - *Keeps for 2 to 3 days in the fridge.*

CATEGORIES - *Indulgent · Entertaining · Quick & easy · Gluten free*

INGREDIENTS

1 tbsp butter

1 shallot, chopped

2 cloves garlic, chopped

¼ cup finely diced chorizo

1 can (4 ½ oz) snails, rinsed and drained

Salt and pepper, to taste

1 tsp maple syrup

¾ cup tomato sauce

1 cup shredded mozzarella cheese

2 tbsp freshly grated Parmesan cheese

STEPS

1   In a pan, over medium heat, melt the butter.
Add the shallot, garlic, and chorizo, and sauté for 2 minutes.
Add the snails, and continue cooking for 1 minute. Season.

2   Add the remaining ingredients, with the exception of
the cheeses, reduce the heat to low, and cook for 2 minutes.
Adjust the seasoning to taste, top with cheeses, and finish by
broiling until golden brown. Serve.

Much as I love peanut sauce, I wanted to try something a little different,
so I used cashews to make a new dip that was just as creamy and delicious.
As for the tartare, I made it with albacore tuna, as opposed to red tuna, since it's
sold at eco-conscious fish markets. Plus, it's way cheaper.

BEST BEFORE

Keeps in individually plastic-wrapped packages for 1 to 2 days in the fridge.

CATEGORIES

Entertaining · Quick & easy · Lactose free

FISH & SEAFOOD

INGREDIENTS

FOR THE CASHEW SAUCE

¾ cup roasted cashews

2 tbsp hoisin sauce

2 tbsp soy sauce

Juice of 1 lemon

¼ cup water

FOR THE TARTARE

14 oz fresh albacore tuna steaks, finely diced

1 avocado, pitted, peeled, and cubed or mashed

Juice of 1 lime

1 tsp sesame oil

3 green onions, finely sliced

Salt and pepper, to taste

FOR THE ROLLS

6 large rice paper sheets

1 ½ cups rice vermicelli, cooked

A handful of fresh cilantro

A handful of red cabbage sprouts

STEPS

1   In a food processor, combine all the cashew sauce ingredients, and process until smooth. Set aside.

2   In a bowl, combine all the tartare ingredients. Set aside.

3   Working with one sheet at a time, dip rice paper in a bowl of warm water for a few seconds, until softened. Carefully spread rice paper out on a flat work surface. Top with some of the rice vermicelli, cilantro, cabbage sprouts, and tartare. Gently fold in the bottom and sides of the rice paper around the toppings. Repeat with the remaining rice paper sheets.

4   Serve the rolls with a generous side of cashew sauce.

TIP

*I recommend not using a wooden cutting board to assemble the rolls, as the rice paper will stick
to it and tear. Instead, use a countertop or large plate.*

TUNA SPRING ROLLS
WITH CASHEW DIPPING SAUCE

QUANTITY : *6 rolls* · 30 MIN · *Doesn't freeze well.*

COD WITH LIME AND COCONUT MILK
& JASMINE RICE

I know it's a boring detail, but I devised this recipe using a whole 400 mL can of coconut milk to avoid waste. It also makes for simpler grocery shopping. One part is used to prepare the cod, and the rest is for the rice.

BEST BEFORE - *Serve immediately.*

CATEGORIES - *Lactose free · Gluten free*

INGREDIENTS

FOR THE RICE

1 ½ cups jasmine rice

Juice of 1 lime

1 cup water

⅔ cup coconut milk

Salt and pepper, to taste

1 tbsp sesame seeds

2 green onions, finely sliced

FOR THE FISH

Dash of olive oil, for cooking

1 red bell pepper, cut into strips

2 green onions, finely sliced

2 cloves garlic, chopped

1 cup coconut milk

½ cup tomato sauce

1 tsp sweet paprika

1 tsp ground cumin

1 tbsp sugar

Zest and juice of 1 lime

Salt and pepper, to taste

14 oz fresh cod, cut into 1-inch cubes

2 tbsp chopped fresh cilantro

STEPS

FOR THE RICE

1   Place the rice in a sieve and rinse a few times.

2   In a pot, combine all the rice ingredients, with the exception of the sesame seeds and green onions. Cover with a lid and bring to a boil. Reduce the heat to low and simmer for 12 minutes.

3   Remove the pan from the heat and set aside for 10 minutes.

4   Add the sesame seeds and green onions. Stir well, and adjust the seasoning to taste. Set aside.

FOR THE FISH

5   In a large pan, over medium heat, heat the olive oil. Add the red pepper, green onions, and garlic, and sauté for 7 to 8 minutes. Stir in the remaining fish ingredients, with the exception of the cod and cilantro. Simmer for 5 minutes.

6   Gently stir in the cod and simmer for another 5 minutes. Stir in the cilantro, and adjust the seasoning to taste. Serve with the rice.

This topping is delicious on shrimp, and if you're an oyster-lover like me,
I suggest trying it on oysters too. Just spoon some on top of fresh oysters and
put them under the broiler for a few minutes until the cheese is melted.
It's "to die for," as my father would say. Incidentally, he loved it so much,
he ate most of what you see in the photo!

ROCKEFELLER-STYLE BUTTERFLY SHRIMP

BEST BEFORE - *Keeps for 2 to 3 days in the fridge.*

CATEGORIES - *Indulgent · Entertaining*

INGREDIENTS

12 to 16 regular or jumbo shrimp (fresh or frozen), deveined and butterflied

Salt and pepper, to taste

FOR THE TOPPING

1 tbsp butter

2 shallots, chopped

2 cloves garlic, chopped

2 tbsp pastis (or dry white wine)

¼ cup 35% cream

4 cups baby spinach

Juice of ½ lemon

Salt and pepper, to taste

4 slices Swiss cheese, cut into quarters

2 tbsp plain breadcrumbs

STEPS

1 In a pan, over medium heat, melt the butter. Add the shallots and garlic, and sauté for 2 minutes. Deglaze the pan with the pastis (or white wine), and simmer for a few minutes, until the liquid has evaporated.

2 Stir in the cream, baby spinach, and lemon juice, and season generously. Cook until the spinach has wilted. Set aside.

3 Preheat the oven to 400°F, with the rack in centre position.

4 Open shrimp and gently press flat, place on a baking sheet, and season. Spoon a bit of topping on top of each shrimp, and then cover with a piece of cheese. Dust with breadcrumbs. Bake for 5 minutes (pre-cooked shrimp) to 10 minutes (raw shrimp).

5 To finish, place pan under broiler and heat until golden brown.

I love versatile recipes that can be served either as an appetizer for a fancy dinner or as a poolside lunch while watching my uncle dance to Enrique Iglesias hits. Oh yeah!

If you're in the mood to make this recipe, take the opportunity to say hello to your local fishmonger. You don't want to take any risks when making a tartare, so you'll want fish of the highest quality.

SALMON TARTARE & ASIAN PEAR CROSTINI

177

BEST BEFORE - *Serve immediately.*

CATEGORIES - *Entertaining · Quick & easy · Lactose free*

FISH & SEAFOOD

INGREDIENTS

½ baguette (or ciabatta bread)

Dash of olive oil

Sprouts or greens of your choice, for garnish (optional)

FOR THE TARTARE

7 oz salmon fillet, skinless (sushi quality)

Half an Asian pear, peeled, cored, and finely diced

2 tbsp mayonnaise

1 ½ tsp Sriracha sauce (see tip below)

2 tsp rice vinegar

Salt and pepper, to taste

STEPS

1   Preheat the oven to 350°F, with the rack in centre position.

2   Cut crostini into 1-inch-thick slices, and arrange on a baking sheet. Sprinkle with olive oil. Bake for 10 minutes.

3   Meanwhile, finely dice the salmon and transfer to a bowl along with the remaining tartare ingredients. Stir well.

4   Top each crostini with tartare, and garnish with greenery. Serve.

TIP

If you don't like a lot of spice, reduce the amount of Sriracha to just a few drops.

At the risk of being judged by readers, I confess I often put potato chips in my burgers and sandwiches. Try it and you'll see it's not the worst idea in the world. Similar to the mayonnaise cake in my first book, I'm sure this recipe will become a classic for many of you.

BEST BEFORE - *Keeps for 1 to 2 days in the fridge.*

CATEGORIES - *Economical · Indulgent · Entertaining · Quick & easy · Lactose free*

INGREDIENTS

6 hamburger buns, split

⅓ cup mayonnaise

Plain potato chips, to taste

FOR THE FISH

Salt and pepper, to taste

6 flounder fillets, skinless (3 ½ oz each)

½ cup all-purpose flour

2 eggs, beaten

1 cup plain panko breadcrumbs

¼ cup vegetable oil, for cooking

FOR THE TOPPING

1 Ataulfo mango, peeled, pitted, and cut into small cubes

2 tbsp capers, rinsed and drained

½ cup chopped cucumber (cut into small cubes)

½ cup chopped tomato (seeded and cut into small cubes)

Juice of ½ lemon

1 tbsp olive oil

Salt and pepper, to taste

1 cup finely sliced Boston lettuce

STEPS

1 In a bowl, combine all the topping ingredients, with the exception of the lettuce. Set aside.

2 Season the fish, and bread them by dredging first in the flour, then the egg, and ending in the breadcrumbs.

3 In a large non-stick pan, over high heat, heat the vegetable oil. Fry the breaded fish for 3 to 4 minutes per side, until golden brown. Remove from the heat, and season. Set aside.

4 Toast the buns and spread with mayonnaise. Top with the fish.

5 Add the lettuce to the topping mixture, and stir well. Spoon some topping onto the fish, and garnish with chips. Serve.

CRISPY FISH BURGERS WITH
MANGO & POTATO CHIP TOPPING

FLAVOURED BUTTER

Here's a simple recipe idea for enhancing just about any dish. All you have to do is prepare the rolls of butter and let them set in the fridge, then slice and store them in the freezer. They're perfect for serving in curls, on corn, in a veggie purée, in mashed potatoes, over pasta, over fish, with meat — the possibilities are endless.

OLIVE, LEMON & ANCHOVY BUTTER

INGREDIENTS

1 cup (½ lb) butter, at room temperature
⅓ cup Kalamata olives, pitted and chopped
2 anchovy fillets, chopped
Zest of ½ lemon

PARMESAN & BACON BUTTER

INGREDIENTS

1 cup (½ lb) butter, at room temperature
4 strips bacon, cooked and chopped
⅓ cup freshly grated Parmesan cheese
1 tbsp grainy mustard

SUNDRIED TOMATO & FRESH HERB BUTTER

INGREDIENTS

1 cup (½ lb) butter, at room temperature
⅓ cup sundried tomatoes in oil, finely chopped
6 to 8 fresh basil leaves, chopped
2 sprigs thyme, leaves only, chopped
2 tbsp chopped fresh cilantro leaves

STEPS

1   In a bowl, combine all the ingredients of the flavour of your choice. Using your hands, shape mixture into a long cylinder. Roll tightly in a piece of plastic wrap.

2   Refrigerate for 2 hours, then slice into rounds.

3   The butter can be frozen for a few months, or kept in the fridge for 2 weeks.

TIP

The butter shouldn't be too soft when it's rolled. If it is, simply let it set for a few minutes in the fridge before rolling.

CHAPTER

No.^{6}

—

MEAT

Meat and I haven't always been best friends. I've just naturally gravitated towards vegetarian dishes. If you'd given me the choice between a big, juicy hamburger and a green salad, I'd have picked the green salad — for no other reason than the taste.

Yet, strangely, ever since Jeanne was born, I've craved meat, to the point of getting excited about cooking a good steak, spare ribs, or chicken in the middle of the week.

It's as if my body needs it. Even though my menus still focus on mostly vegetarian dishes, I've discovered my carnivorous side and I love it.

I've found a good balance. Also, visiting my local butcher is probably the coolest thing I do. Seeing people who are equally passionate about their life's work inspired many recipes in this section, which I'm more fond of than I would have expected.

MOUSSAKA

QUANTITY : *8–10 servings* · ⚭ 30 MIN · ◷ 1 H 45 · ☾ 45 MIN · *Freezes well.*

BEST BEFORE - *Keeps for 3 to 4 days in the fridge.*

CATEGORIES - *Entertaining · Indulgent*

CONTINUED ON PAGE 186

CONTINUED FROM PAGE 184

INGREDIENTS

FOR THE EGGPLANT

*2 medium eggplants (about 6 cups),
cut into 1 cm rounds*

⅓ cup olive oil

Salt and pepper, to taste

*4 cups peeled and sliced (¼ inch thick)
yellow potatoes*

FOR THE MEAT MIXTURE

1 tbsp olive oil

1 yellow onion, chopped

1 lb ground lamb (or ground beef)

2 cloves garlic, chopped

Salt and pepper, to taste

1 tsp ground allspice

1 can (28 oz) crushed tomatoes

¼ cup chopped fresh parsley

1 bay leaf

2 egg whites

FOR THE BÉCHAMEL

¼ cup butter

⅓ cup all-purpose flour

2 ½ cups milk

2 egg yolks

½ cup freshly grated Parmesan cheese

Salt and pepper, to taste

MEAT

FOR THE EGGPLANT

1   Arrange the eggplant in a single layer
    on a baking sheet. Brush with olive
    oil and season.

2   With the rack in the middle of
    the oven, broil the eggplant for
    15 minutes. Set aside.

FOR THE MEAT MIXTURE

3   In a pot, over high heat, heat the
    olive oil. Add the onion, and sauté
    for 2 minutes, or until tender. Add
    the ground meat and the garlic, and
    continue cooking for 5 minutes.
    Season. Stir in the remaining
    ingredients, with the exception of the
    egg whites. Reduce the heat to low
    and simmer for 20 minutes. Remove
    from the heat and let the sauce cool
    for 30 minutes (very important).

4   Once the sauce is cool, add the
    egg whites and stir well. Adjust the
    seasoning to taste (it's important that
    it be well salted).

FOR THE BÉCHAMEL

5   In another pot, melt the butter.
    Stir in the flour to create a batter,
    and cook, stirring, for 1 minute.

6   Gradually add ½ cup of the milk,
    whisking to avoid lumps. Slowly
    incorporate the remaining milk,
    whisking constantly, and bring
    to a boil.

7   Remove the pan from the heat and let
    cool for 15 minutes (very important).
    Add the egg yolks and the Parmesan,
    and stir well. Season and set aside.

FOR THE ASSEMBLY

8   Preheat the oven to 350°F. Grease a
    10-inch × 14-inch baking sheet.

9   Arrange the eggplant and potato
    slices in an alternating pattern on the
    baking sheet. Cover with the meat
    mixture and the béchamel sauce.
    Bake, uncovered, for 1 hour.

CHICKEN BREASTS IN CILANTRO SAUCE WITH TOMATO QUINOA

QUANTITY : *2 servings* · 🥄 15 MIN · 🕐 40 MIN · *Freezes well.*

BEST BEFORE - *Keeps for 2 to 3 days in the fridge.*

CATEGORIES - *Entertaining · Lactose free · Gluten free*

PHOTO ON PAGE 188

TIP

You can find roasted red peppers in the condiments section of most grocery stores.

INGREDIENTS

Salt and pepper, to taste

2 boneless, skinless chicken breasts

1 tsp maple syrup

1 tsp sweet paprika

1 tbsp vegetable oil

FOR THE PEPPER SAUCE

*½ cup store-bought roasted red peppers
(see tip below)*

½ cup chopped fresh cilantro

½ cup chopped fresh parsley

Juice of 2 limes

1 tbsp maple syrup

¼ cup olive oil

Salt and pepper, to taste

FOR THE QUINOA

½ cup quinoa

1 can (19 oz) tomato juice

1 tsp sweet paprika

Salt and pepper, to taste

STEPS

1   In a food processor, combine all the pepper sauce ingredients, and process until smooth. Set aside in the fridge.

2   Preheat the oven to 400°F, with the rack in centre position.

3   Season the chicken breasts. Using a brush, or your fingertips, slather them with maple syrup and paprika.

4   In a large pan, over high heat, heat the vegetable oil. Sear the chicken breasts for 1 to 2 minutes per side, until browned. Transfer to an oven-safe dish, and bake for 20 minutes, or until cooked through.

5   Meanwhile, combine all the quinoa ingredients in a pot. Bring to a boil, reduce the heat to low, and simmer for 15 minutes. Adjust the seasoning to taste. Slice the chicken and serve with the sauce.

191

TO BARBEQUE

Heat the barbeque on high, grease the grill, and sear the chicken on both sides. Then reduce the heat to medium, transfer the chicken to the uppermost grill, close the lid, and cook for 20 minutes, or until cooked through.

You can also cook the quinoa in a pot on the barbeque's side grill.

HIS CHOICE

TERIYAKI CHICKEN AND VERMICELLI WITH GINGER & BASIL PESTO

BEST BEFORE - *Keeps for 2 to 3 days in the fridge.*

CATEGORIES - *Quick & easy · Lactose free · Gluten free*

192

MEAT

INGREDIENTS

1 tbsp vegetable oil

8 boneless, skinless chicken thighs, quartered

4 servings rice vermicelli

FOR THE SAUCE

1 tbsp cornstarch diluted in 1 tbsp water

¼ cup soy sauce

¼ cup brown sugar

2 tbsp rice vinegar

1 clove garlic, chopped

1 tbsp sesame seeds

Salt and pepper, to taste

FOR THE PESTO

3 tbsp minced peeled fresh ginger

⅓ cup olive oil

½ cup fresh basil leaves

1 tbsp peanut butter

1 tbsp rice vinegar

1 tsp Sriracha sauce (optional)

STEPS

1 In a food processor, combine all the pesto ingredients, and process until smooth. Set aside.

2 In a bowl, combine all the sauce ingredients. Set aside.

3 In a pan, over high heat, heat the vegetable oil. Add the chicken, and sauté for 5 minutes. Stir in the sauce, reduce the heat to medium, and continue cooking for 5 more minutes, or until the chicken is completely cooked through. Adjust the seasoning to taste, and set aside.

4 Cook the rice vermicelli according to the package directions. Drain, and transfer to a bowl. Add the pesto, and stir until well coated.

5 Serve the vermicelli with the chicken.

Some people love meatloaf that's more sweet than "tomato-y," and others prefer it more "tomato-y" than sweet. Nice person that I am, I created a meatloaf that is perfectly balanced between the two. I'm convinced that this is one recipe that both types of meatloaf lovers will adore, and that consequently it will go a long way to achieving world peace. I become short of breath just thinking about all the problems we can solve with this book.

CLASSIC MEATLOAF

BEST BEFORE - *Keeps for 2 to 3 days in the fridge.*

CATEGORIES - *Economical · Lactose free*

INGREDIENTS

STEPS

FOR THE MEATLOAF

1 tbsp butter

2 cloves garlic, chopped

1 package (5 oz) baby spinach

2 carrots, cut lengthwise

1 yellow onion, quartered

1 ¾ lbs ground beef

1 cup quick-cooking oats

1 egg

2 tsp chili powder

¼ tsp salt

Black pepper, to taste

FOR THE SAUCE

2 ½ cups tomato sauce

¾ cup brown sugar

⅓ cup balsamic vinegar

3 tbsp Dijon mustard

1   Preheat the oven to 350°F, with the rack in centre position.

2   In a bowl, combine all the sauce ingredients. Set aside.

3   In a pan, over medium heat, melt the butter. Add the garlic, and sauté for 2 minutes. Add the spinach, and sauté until wilted. Season, and remove from heat. Set aside.

4   In a food processor, finely chop the carrots and onion. Add the spinach, and pulse a few times until roughly chopped. Transfer the mixture to a bowl, and add the remaining meatloaf ingredients. Add ½ cup of sauce, and stir well.

5   Using your hands, shape the mixture into a loaf about 12-inches × 4-inches and place in a roasting pan. Pour the remaining sauce over top. Bake for 1 hour. Serve.

BEEF CARPACCIO WITH ARUGULA VINAIGRETTE & PARMESAN WHIPPED CREAM

QUANTITY : *4 appetizers or 2 mains* · 🥄 20 MIN · *Doesn't freeze well.*

I declare myself queen of whipped creams, or star of stiff peaks, whichever you prefer. My humility totally goes out the window when it comes to this Parmesan whipped cream. It's so good I pat myself on the back whenever I think of it. I didn't even want to do a Google search to see if anyone else had already thought of it (which seems obvious), because I want to continue to believe I invented it. It's delicious served over this classic carpaccio dish, and probably over anything else. I'd spread it on toast — you get the idea.

BEST BEFORE - *Serve immediately.*

CATEGORIES - *Entertaining · Quick & easy*

INGREDIENTS

7 oz very fresh beef sirloin

Salt and pepper, to taste

¼ cup pecans, roasted and chopped

A few small bread slices, fresh or toasted

FOR THE VINAIGRETTE

1 cup finely chopped arugula

2 tbsp white balsamic vinegar

1 tsp Dijon mustard

¼ cup olive oil

Salt, to taste

FOR THE WHIPPED CREAM

½ cup 35% cream

½ cup freshly grated Parmesan cheese

Black pepper, to taste

STEPS

1 In a small bowl, combine all the vinaigrette ingredients. Set aside in the fridge until ready to serve.

2 Using a whisk or electric mixer, whip the cream until stiff peaks form, then mix in the Parmesan and the pepper. Cover and refrigerate.

3 Slice the beef as finely as possible, and lay it out on a serving platter. Season.

4 Drizzle the beef with the vinaigrette, and top with the whipped cream and pecans. Serve immediately with the bread.

ROASTED DRUMSTICKS
WITH RED ONION MAYONNAISE

BEST BEFORE - *Keeps for 2 to 3 days in the fridge.*

CATEGORIES - *Economical · Indulgent · Lactose free · Gluten free*

INGREDIENTS

8 skin-on chicken drumsticks

2 cups small new potatoes, halved

3 cups peeled and cubed (1 inch) butternut squash

2 sprigs rosemary, leaves only

½ red onion, finely sliced

2 tbsp balsamic vinegar

¼ cup olive oil

Salt and pepper, to taste

FOR THE MAYONNAISE

1 tbsp butter

½ red onion, chopped

1 tbsp balsamic vinegar

½ cup mayonnaise

FOR THE SEASONING

1 tbsp brown sugar

½ tsp salt

1 tsp onion powder

1 tsp sweet paprika

1 tsp ground fennel seeds

STEPS

FOR THE MAYONNAISE

1   In a small pot, over medium heat, melt the butter. Add the onion, and sauté until golden brown. Add the balsamic vinegar, and stir well. Transfer to a bowl and let cool completely in the fridge. Once cool, add the mayonnaise, and stir well. Set aside.

FOR THE BAKING SHEET

2   Preheat the oven to 400°F, with the rack in centre position.

3   In a bowl, combine all the seasoning ingredients. Add the drumsticks, and stir well. Set aside.

4   On a large baking sheet, combine the potatoes, squash, rosemary, onion, balsamic vinegar, and olive oil, and season generously.

5   Place the drumsticks on the baking sheet among the vegetables, and bake for 45 minutes, stirring halfway through. Serve with the delicious mayonnaise.

MEAT

BEST BEFORE - *Keeps for 2 to 3 days in the fridge.*

CATEGORIES - *Quick & easy · Lactose free · Gluten free*

INGREDIENTS

14 to 21 oz flank steak

FOR THE MARINADE

3 tbsp balsamic vinegar

2 tbsp soy sauce (or tamari)

2 tbsp Worcestershire sauce

2 tbsp vegetable oil

2 tbsp grainy mustard

3 cloves garlic, chopped

1 tsp salt

FOR THE PEPPERS

12 to 16 small sweet bell peppers

1 tbsp balsamic vinegar

1 tbsp vegetable oil

1 clove garlic, chopped

Salt and pepper, to taste

STEPS

1 Using a toothpick, prick the steak all over (this will allow the marinade to saturate the meat).

2 In a large resealable bag, combine all the marinade ingredients. Add the steak, and turn to coat. Refrigerate for a minimum of 2 hours, or a maximum of 36 hours.

3 Preheat the oven to 400°F, with the rack in centre position.

4 In a bowl, combine all the pepper ingredients. Arrange peppers in a single layer on a baking sheet. Set aside.

5 Heat a dry pan over high heat. Sear the steak for 2 minutes per side, or until golden brown; reserve the marinade. Transfer to the baking sheet with the peppers, and bake for 14 minutes (or until cooked to your taste).

6 Let the steak rest for 5 minutes. Meanwhile, pour the marinade into the same pan used for the steak, and boil for a few minutes. Set aside.

7 Slice the steak against the grain of the meat, and serve with the peppers and the sauce.

TO BARBECUE

Heat the barbeque on high, and sear the steak on both sides. Then reduce the heat to medium, and continue cooking to desired doneness. You can also grill the peppers over medium heat for 8 to 10 minutes.

QUANTITY : *2–4* · 🥄 10 MIN · ⏱ 25 MIN · ☾ 2–36 H · *Freezes well.*

ASIAN-STYLE PORK-STUFFED BUNS WITH CREAMY CUCUMBER TOPPING

BEST BEFORE - *Keeps for 2 to 3 days in the fridge.*

CATEGORIES - *Economical · Quick & easy · Lactose free*

203

INGREDIENTS

4 to 6 hot dog buns or 12 stuffable rolls

FOR THE STUFFING

Dash of vegetable oil, for cooking

1 lb ground pork

2 green onions, finely sliced

2 cloves garlic, chopped

2 tbsp chopped peeled fresh ginger

Salt and pepper, to taste

¼ cup hoisin sauce

¼ cup soy sauce

Juice of 1 lime

1 to 2 tsp Sriracha sauce, to taste

FOR THE TOPPING

*2 tbsp chopped fresh cilantro
(or mint or Thai basil)*

1 cup diced cucumber

2 tsp mayonnaise

1 tsp rice vinegar

Salt and pepper, to taste

STEPS

1 In a pan, over medium heat, heat a dash of vegetable oil. Add the ground pork, green onions, garlic, and ginger, and sauté for 5 minutes. Season.

2 Stir in the remaining stuffing ingredients, and continue cooking for 5 minutes. Adjust the seasoning, and set aside.

3 In a bowl, combine all the topping ingredients. Set aside.

4 Warm or toast the buns, and fill with the meat and the topping. Serve.

MEAT

HIS CHOICE

RIBS WITH HOMEMADE BARBEQUE SAUCE

204

MEAT

BEST BEFORE

Keeps for 2 to 3 days in the fridge.

CATEGORIES

*Indulgent · Entertaining
Lactose free · Gluten free*

INGREDIENTS

*¾ cup homemade barbeque sauce
(see recipe on page 207)*

FOR THE RIBS

1 or 2 racks of ribs

¼ cup sugar

2 tbsp salt

1 tbsp whole black peppercorns

*½ cup homemade or store-bought
unsweetened applesauce*

1 yellow onion, minced

2 to 4 litres water

STEPS

FOR OVEN COOKING

1 Prepare the barbecue sauce (see recipe on page 207).

2 In a large pot, combine the ribs ingredients. The water should just cover the ribs.

3 Bring to a boil, reduce the heat to low, and simmer for 1 ½ hours. Drain the meat.

4 Preheat the oven to 400°F, with the rack in centre position.

5 Slather both sides of the ribs with a generous amount of sauce, and place on a baking sheet. Bake for 30 minutes.

6 Brush the meat with sauce again. To finish, broil the ribs until the sauce caramelizes.

FOR BARBEQUING

1 Prepare the barbecue sauce (see recipe on page 207).

2 In a large pot, combine all the ribs ingredients. The water should just cover the ribs.

3 Bring to a boil, reduce the heat to low, and simmer for 1 ½ hours. Drain the meat.

4 Heat the barbecue on medium. Place the ribs on the upper grill, and slather with sauce. Cook, with the lid closed, for 20 to 25 minutes, until the sauce is nicely caramelized.

Making extra homemade barbeque sauce should be automatic
for everyone, at the first signs of summer.

It only takes a few minutes to prepare and will keep for over 6 months in
the fridge. It'll save more than a few improvised meals, believe me.

QUANTITY : *25 oz* · ✎ 1 0 MIN · 🕐 3 0 MIN · ☾ 1 H · *Freezes well.*

HOMEMADE BARBECUE SAUCE

BEST BEFORE - *Keeps for 6 months in the fridge.*

CATEGORIES - *Lactose free · Gluten free · Gift · Entertaining*

INGREDIENTS

1 yellow onion, quartered

2 cloves garlic, minced

*1 cup homemade or store-bought
    unsweetened applesauce*

½ cup red wine vinegar

¼ cup Worcestershire sauce

1 cup brown sugar

¾ cup molasses

1 can (5 ½ oz) tomato paste

2 tsp sambal oelek

1 tsp ground allspice

1 tsp smoked paprika

1 tsp salt

STEPS

1   In a pot, whisk together all the
    ingredients. Bring to a boil, reduce the
    heat to low, and simmer for 30 minutes.

2   Strain the mixture through a sieve to
    remove the onion. Let cool for 1 hour,
    until the sauce thickens.

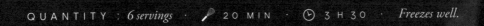

QUANTITY : *6 servings* · 🥄 20 MIN · 🕐 3 H 30 · *Freezes well.*

BEEF BLADE ROAST WITH ROOT VEGETABLES & HERB ANCHOÏADE

INGREDIENTS

FOR THE ROAST

Salt and pepper, to taste

2 boneless beef blades (about 1 ½ lbs each)

2 tbsp vegetable oil

1 yellow onion, finely sliced

½ cup red wine

1 cup beef broth

1 tbsp tomato paste

4 sprigs fresh thyme

FOR THE VEGETABLES

*1 celeriac, peeled, quartered, and sliced
    into 2 cm pieces*

6 carrots, peeled and cut lengthwise

FOR THE HERB ANCHOÏADE

1 green onion, cut lengthwise

5 anchovy fillets

1 clove garlic, halved

2 tsp capers, drained

Zest and juice of 1 lemon

½ cup fresh parsley

¼ cup vegetable oil

Salt and pepper, to taste

STEPS

1   Preheat the oven to 300°F, with the rack in centre position.

2   Generously season the beef.

3   In a pan, over high heat, heat the vegetable oil. Sear the beef blades on each side until nicely browned. Transfer to a large oven-safe dish. Add the remaining roast ingredients, and season. Cover the baking dish with aluminum foil, or a lid, and bake for 2 hours.

4   Add the vegetables, cover, and continue cooking for 1 ½ hours.

5   Meanwhile, in a food processor, combine all the herb anchoïade ingredients, and process until smooth. Set aside.

6   Just before serving, drizzle the dish with the herb anchoïade.

209

MEAT

TIP

To make this in a slow cooker, cook on High for 6 hours or Low for 8 hours. Sear the meat before adding to the slow cooker. Add the vegetables halfway through the cooking time.

CHAPTER

No.7

—

PASTA, RICE & PIZZA

HOMEMADE COLD PIZZA

RECIPE ON PAGE 214

HOMEMADE COLD PIZZA

PHOTO ON PAGE 212

BEST BEFORE - *Keeps for 3 to 4 days in the fridge.*

CATEGORIES - *Gift · Economical · Entertaining · Lactose free*

When I was younger, my mother really didn't have a lot of money. Years later, she told me that we'd often have supper at my aunts' houses, on nights when the fridge, and her wallet, were bare. I never suffered, proving that children can pretty much survive on love alone. I'd even go so far to say that the only impact it had on my childhood was to allow me to develop an intimate relationship with cold pizza from the grocery store. We ate it all the time. It was inexpensive, and my brother and I loved it. My mother served it alongside a bag of baby carrots with a ketchup and mayonnaise dip, and we were in heaven.

QUANTITY : *1 pizza* · 🥄 20 MIN · 🕐 20 MIN · 🌙 2 H · *Freezes well.*

INGREDIENTS

1 portion pizza dough, homemade
or store-bought (see tips below)

FOR THE SAUCE

1 can (28 oz) diced tomatoes, drained

2 tbsp tomato paste

¼ cup sundried tomatoes, chopped

3 anchovy fillets, chopped

1 shallot, chopped

2 cloves garlic, chopped

1 tbsp chopped fresh oregano

¼ cup olive oil

1 tsp sugar

Salt and pepper, to taste

STEPS

1   Preheat the oven to 425°F, with the rack in centre position.

2   Grease a 10-inch × 14-inch baking sheet, and put the pizza dough on it. Cover with plastic wrap, and set aside in a warm place for 1 hour to let the dough rise.

3   In a bowl, combine all the sauce ingredients. Set aside.

4   Using your fingers, gently spread the dough out to fill the baking sheet, pressing down to form small cavities and to help it deflate a little. Spread all the sauce evenly over the top of the dough, and bake for 20 minutes.

5   Let cool completely before cutting and serving.

TIPS

There's a good pizza dough recipe in my first book. I also suggest buying tomato paste in tubes rather than small cans. It'll keep a hundred times better.

CREAMY TUNA LINGUINE

QUANTITY : *2 servings* · 🥄 5 MIN · 🕐 10 MIN · *Doesn't freeze well.*

BEST BEFORE - *Keeps for 2 to 3 days in the fridge.*

CATEGORIES - *Economical · Quick & easy*

INGREDIENTS

2 servings linguine pasta

1 tbsp olive oil

1 clove garlic, chopped

1 zucchini, halved and cut into half rounds

1 can (6 oz) chunked light tuna in water

½ tsp smoked paprika

½ cup water

¾ cup sour cream

½ cup shredded aged cheddar cheese

Salt and pepper, to taste

STEPS

1   Bring a large pot of salted water to a boil. Cook the pasta according to the package directions. Drain, and set aside.

2   In a large pan, over medium heat, heat the olive oil. Add the garlic and zucchini, and sauté for 4 minutes. Stir in the tuna and paprika, and continue cooking for 1 minute.

3   Add the water, sour cream, and cheddar, and stir until smooth and creamy.

4   Add the pasta, stir well, season, and serve.

BEEF ROTINI & CHEDDAR
CHEESE CASSEROLE

This is a fusion between beef macaroni and cheese macaroni, just like our grandmothers used to make. It's simply heavenly.

I know it'd be better with vegetables added, but I wanted to keep the recipe super simple and in a version everyone would like. However, don't hesitate to add vegetables of your choice.

It's normal for there to be a lot of sauce. Oven-baked pasta tends to soak up sauce to the point that it becomes dry the next day, so I wasn't shy about adding it

Keeps for 1 week in the fridge.

CATEGORIES

Economical · Indulgent · Entertaining

INGREDIENTS

8 cups rotini

2 cups shredded mozzarella cheese

FOR THE MEAT

1 tbsp olive oil

1 yellow onion, chopped

2 cloves garlic, chopped

450 g ground beef

Salt and pepper, to taste

1 can (5 ½ oz) tomato paste

1 can (28 oz) diced tomatoes

1 can (28 oz) crushed tomatoes

1 tbsp dried Italian herb mix

FOR THE CHEESE SAUCE

¼ cup butter

⅓ cup all-purpose flour

2 tbsp Dijon mustard

3 cups milk

2 cups shredded cheddar cheese

Salt and pepper, to taste

STEPS

FOR THE MEAT

1   In a pot, over medium heat, heat the olive oil. Add the onion and garlic, and sauté until softened. Add the ground beef, and continue cooking until cooked through. Season.

2   Add the remaining meat ingredients, stir well, and season again. Cover, reduce the heat to low, and simmer for 20 minutes. Set aside.

FOR THE CHEESE SAUCE

3   In a pot, over medium heat, melt the butter. Add the flour and mustard. Whisk until a paste is formed.

4   Add 1 cup of milk, whisking continually to avoid lumps. Gradually add the remaining milk, still whisking constantly, and bring to a boil. Add the cheddar, whisk well, and season. Set aside.

ASSEMBLY

5   Bring a large pot of water to a boil. Cook the pasta for 1 minute less than indicated on the package directions. Drain, and set aside.

6   Preheat the oven to 350°F, with the rack in centre position.

7   In a baking dish, alternate layers of meat mixture, cheese sauce, and pasta. Finish with a layer of cheese sauce and top with mozzarella.

8   Bake for 30 minutes. To finish, broil until the cheese is nicely browned.

BEST BEFORE - *Keeps for 3 to 4 days in the fridge.*

CATEGORIES - *Economical · Lactose free · Gluten free · Vegetarian*

INGREDIENTS

1 tbsp butter

4 eggs

2 cups grated raw zucchini

FOR THE RICE

1 ½ cups basmati rice

2 ¼ cups water

1 tbsp sugar

1 tbsp rice vinegar

FOR THE TOFU IN SAUCE

Dash of olive oil

4 green onions, finely sliced

2 cloves garlic, chopped

1 tbsp chopped peeled fresh ginger

1 package (4 oz) fresh shiitake mushrooms, finely sliced

1 package (1 lb) firm tofu, cut into ½ cm dice

2 tbsp tomato sauce

⅓ cup soy sauce (or tamari)

3 tbsp rice vinegar

1 tsp sesame oil

1 ¼ cups water

2 tbsp cornstarch diluted in 2 tbsp water

1 to 2 tsp sambal oelek, to taste

Salt and pepper, to taste

STEPS

1   Rinse the rice a few times under cold water. Drain well.

2   In a pot, combine all the rice ingredients, and bring to a boil. Reduce the heat to low, cover, and simmer for 12 minutes. Remove the pan from the heat, and set aside.

3   In a large pan, over medium heat, heat the olive oil. Add the green onions, garlic, ginger, and shiitakes, and sauté for 8 minutes. Add the remaining tofu in sauce ingredients, reduce the heat to low, and simmer for 5 minutes. Adjust the seasoning to taste, and set aside.

4   In a small pan, over medium heat, melt the butter. Cook the eggs sunny side up (without flipping). Set aside.

5   In a bowl, serve the tofu in sauce over rice, and top with an egg and grated zucchini.

BASMATI RICE BOWL WITH SWEET AND
SOUR TOFU & EGGS SUNNY SIDE UP

It's impossible not to be in a good mood when you're sitting in front of a plate of long macaroni. In any event, eating bucatini brings me joy. Party poopers (I'm not exaggerating!) can easily replace it with linguine, spaghetti, or any other type of pasta (good-quality fresh pasta is available in specialty stores, and is definitely worth trying if you haven't already).

I wanted to make a sauce that was super quick and easy, and didn't involve cooking, cream, or cheese, but feel free to tailor the recipe to your tastes by adding one of those ingredients without worrying about ruining the whole thing.

For my money, I'd be willing to bet this recipe will be a hit among the kids in your life.

LONG MACARONI WITH FRESH & SUNDRIED TOMATOES

BEST BEFORE

Keeps for 1 week in the fridge.

CATEGORIES

Quick & easy · Lactose free · Vegetarian

INGREDIENTS

4 servings long macaroni (or bucatini)

½ cup hot water, reserved from the cooked pasta

Salt and pepper, to taste

FOR THE SAUCE

1 tbsp olive oil

¼ cup pine nuts

¼ cup sundried tomatoes in oil

1 medium tomato, quartered

½ cup jarred artichokes, drained

5 to 6 fresh basil leaves

1 tsp sugar

Salt and pepper, to taste

STEPS

1   In a small pan, over medium heat, heat the olive oil. Toast the pine nuts, stirring constantly. Transfer to a food processor, along with the remaining sauce ingredients, and process until smooth. Set aside.

2   Bring a large pot of salted water to a boil, and cook the pasta according to the package directions. Reserve ½ cup of the cooking water, drain pasta, and set aside.

3   In a pan, add the sauce, the reserved pasta water, and the pasta. Season.

4   Cook over medium heat for 2 to 3 minutes, or until the sauce coats the pasta nicely. Adjust the seasoning to taste, and serve.

QUANTITY : *4 servings* · 🥄 10 MIN · ⏲ 15 MIN · *Freezes well.*

TAGLIATELLE WITH GREEN PEA, BACON & FETA PESTO

BEST BEFORE - *Keeps for 3 to 4 days in the fridge.*

CATEGORIES - *Economical · Quick & easy*

INGREDIENTS

4 servings tagliatelle

8 strips bacon, finely sliced

½ cup crumbled feta cheese

FOR THE PESTO

1 cup green peas (thawed if frozen)

½ cup fresh basil

Juice of ½ lemon

¼ cup pine nuts (or walnuts)

½ cup freshly grated Parmesan cheese

⅓ cup olive oil

2 tbsp water

Black pepper, to taste

STEPS

1   In a food processor, combine all the pesto ingredients, and process until smooth. Set aside.

2   Bring a large pot of salted water to a boil, and cook the pasta according to the package directions. Just before cooking finishes, reserve a bit of the pasta cooking water in a glass and set aside. Drain the pasta, and set aside.

3   In a pan, over medium-high heat, sauté the bacon until nice and crispy. Drain the excess grease from the pan. Add the pesto and the pasta, and stir well. Adjust the texture of the sauce to taste by adding a bit of the pasta water.

4   Serve with the feta cheese.

TIP

For a rich and creamy version of this recipe, add ¼ cup 35% cream to the pan at the same time as the pesto.

I probably hold the world record for eating the most pizza pockets. When I was in elementary school, pizza pockets constituted 95% of my lunches, to my mother's great dismay, as she couldn't suggest anything else without me having a nervous breakdown.

How many times have I taken a big bite out of a pizza pocket, only to give my tongue second-degree burns or land on a still-frozen centre? Long live the microwave! Such fond memories.

Now, I present to you a classic childhood dish that you're certain to fall in love with. There are tons of ideas for fillings, so have fun. Just remember that your filling shouldn't be too runny. Here are a few suggestions:

GOAT CHEESE, SPINACH & FRESH TOMATO
PULLED PORK & OLD CHEDDAR
COOKED CHICKEN, CREAM CHEESE & STEAMED BROCCOLI
TOMATO SAUCE, GROUND BEEF & CHEESE
EGGPLANT, TOMATO SAUCE, OLIVES & FETA CHEESE

BEST BEFORE - *Keeps for 1 week in the fridge.*

CATEGORIES - *Economical · Indulgent*

CONTINUED ON PAGE 228

HOMEMADE PIZZA POCKETS

QUANTITY : *12 pockets* · 🥄 40 MIN · ⏱ 35 MIN · ☾ 3 H · *Freezes well after cooking.*

CONTINUED FROM PAGE 226

INGREDIENTS

FOR THE DOUGH

1 cup milk

1 packet (¼ oz) or 2 tsp instant yeast

2 tbsp butter, melted

1 egg, beaten

2 tbsp sugar

2 ¾ cups all-purpose flour

¼ tsp salt

FOR THE TOPPING

1 tbsp olive oil

*1 package (8 oz) button mushrooms,
finely sliced*

*3 ½ oz pepperoni (or other cold cut of your
choice), finely sliced*

1 clove garlic, chopped

1 cup tomato sauce

1 tsp dried oregano

Salt and pepper, to taste

*1 cup cubed mozzarella cheese (or other cheese
of your choice)*

¼ cup milk, for assembly

TIP

*Once cooked and cooled, the pizza pockets can be frozen. To defrost them in the microwave, just wrap
them in paper towel (like in the good old days) and heat.*

FOR THE DOUGH

1 Pour the milk into a small bowl and microwave just until lukewarm. Add the yeast, stir, and let sit for 10 minutes to activate the yeast.

2 In a large bowl, combine the milk mixture with the remaining dough ingredients. Using your hands, form into a ball and knead for 5 minutes. Place the dough back in the bowl, cover with plastic wrap, and place in the oven with the light on. Let sit for 2 hours.

FOR THE TOPPING

3 Meanwhile, in a pan, over medium-high heat, heat the olive oil. Cook the mushrooms for about 5 minutes, or until golden. Stir in the pepperoni and garlic, and continue cooking for 2 minutes. Stir in the tomato sauce and oregano, reduce the heat to medium, and cook for 5 more minutes.

4 Season generously, remove the pan from the heat, and let cool completely (important).

5 Add the cheese cubes, and stir well.

6 Beware! The mixture shouldn't be too runny. If that's the case, drain some sauce.

ASSEMBLY

7 Preheat the oven to 400°F, with the rack in centre position. Line a baking sheet with parchment paper. Set aside.

8 On a floured work surface, roll the dough until 3 mm thick. Cut out rounds 12 cm in diameter. Top each round with about 3 tbsp of the meat mixture.

9 Fold the dough over, to form a pocket. Pinch edges to seal tightly and place pockets (seam side down) on the baking sheet.

10 Brush the pizza pockets with milk, and bake for 20 minutes.

SHELLS WITH CHICKEN
PUTTANESCA & OLIVE SAUCE

HIS
CHOICE

QUANTITY : *4 servings* · ✎ 5 MIN · ⏱ 25 MIN · *The sauce freezes well.*

BEST BEFORE - *Keeps for 3 to 4 days in the fridge.*

CATEGORIES - *Economical · Quick & easy · Lactose free*

INGREDIENTS

5 cups store-bought short pasta (I used medium shells)

¼ cup olive oil

2 boneless, skinless chicken breasts, cubed

2 cloves garlic, minced

3 green onions, finely sliced

2 anchovy fillets, chopped (see tip below)

2 tbsp capers, drained and chopped

1 cup store-bought tomato sauce

½ cup Kalamata olives in oil, drained, pitted, and chopped

6 cups baby spinach

¼ cup chopped fresh parsley

1 tbsp chopped fresh oregano

Black pepper, to taste

STEPS

1   Bring a large pot of salted water to a boil, and cook the shells according to the package directions. Drain, and set aside.

2   In a large pan, over high heat, heat the olive oil. Add the chicken, and cook, undisturbed, for 5 minutes, or until golden. Add the garlic, green onions, anchovies, and capers, and continue cooking for 5 minutes.

3   Add the remaining ingredients, reduce the heat to low, and simmer, stirring, for 5 minutes.

4   Add the pasta, stir well, adjust the seasoning to taste, and serve.

PASTA, RICE & PIZZA

TIP

You can omit the anchovies from this recipe, but I strongly suggest you don't. No one will be able to pick out the flavour, and they add that little something that makes all the difference. Buy a tube of anchovy paste for a longer best before date, and substitute 1 tsp of paste for the fillets.

LEY RISOTTO WITH TOMATOES, DUCK CONFIT & BOCCONCINI

BEST BEFORE - *Keeps for 3 to 4 days in the fridge.*

CATEGORIES - *Indulgent · Entertaining*

232

INGREDIENTS

Meat from 2 store-bought confit duck thighs

2 tbsp butter

1 yellow onion, chopped

Salt and pepper, to taste

¾ cup pearl barley

4 sprigs fresh thyme

1 ½ cups chicken broth

1 ½ cups tomato juice

¼ cup orange juice (see tip below)

1 ½ cups cherry tomatoes, halved

1 ball (about 7 oz) bocconcini cheese (fresh mozzarella), cubed

⅓ cup roasted pecans, chopped

STEPS

1   Loosely shred the duck meat, and set aside.

2   In a pot, over medium heat, melt the butter. Add the onion, and sauté for 5 minutes. Season. Add the barley and thyme, and continue cooking, stirring, for 1 minute.

3   Add the chicken broth, tomato juice, shredded duck, and orange juice. Season again. Cover, reduce the heat to low, and cook for 20 minutes, stirring occasionally.

4   By this time, the barley should be firm but tender to the bite. If the barley is slightly undercooked, add a little water and continue cooking until tender.

5   Stir in the tomatoes, and adjust seasoning to taste. Serve with the bocconcini and pecans.

TIP

If you're not an orange juice lover (although I highly recommend it because it goes so well with duck), substitute an equal amount of chicken broth.

LINGUINE WITH GLAZED PEPPERS & SHRIMP

BEST BEFORE - *Keeps for 2 to 3 days in the fridge.*

CATEGORIES - *Entertaining · Lactose free*

INGREDIENTS

⅓ cup good-quality olive oil

1 red bell pepper, seeded and cut into thin strips

1 orange bell pepper, seeded and cut into thin strips

1 yellow bell pepper, seeded and cut into thin strips

1 yellow onion, finely chopped

2 cloves garlic, chopped

Salt and pepper, to taste

½ cup dry white wine

1 tsp sugar

1 cup raw shrimp, peeled and deveined

4 servings linguine

Freshly grated Parmesan cheese, to taste (optional)

STEPS

1   In a pot, over medium-low heat, combine the olive oil, peppers, onion, and garlic. Season generously, cover, and cook for 30 minutes, stirring occasionally.

2   Add the white wine and sugar, cover, and continue cooking for 10 minutes.

3   Add the shrimp, and cook for 2 to 3 minutes. Season again, and set aside.

4   In another pot, cook the linguine according to the package directions. Drain, and add to the sauce. Continue cooking the pasta for 1 minute. Serve with the Parmesan.

PASTA, RICE & PIZZA

TIP

You can use pre-cooked shrimp, just omit cooking for 2 to 3 minutes in step 3.

QUANTITY : *4 servings* · 🥄 20 MIN · 🕐 1–3 MIN
☾ 30 MIN · *Freezes well (see Tips & Tricks on page 239).*

HOMEMADE FRESH PASTA
(WITH WHOLE WHEAT)

Giving myself an Italian name and making fresh pasta while listening
to music that's a little too loud is one of my favourite activities. So here's
a recipe for fresh pasta that's a perfect compromise between white pasta,
which isn't very nutritious, and whole-wheat pasta, which I always find
tastes too much like whole wheat.

Sincerely, Mariana Lucia

BEST BEFORE - *The ball of dough keeps for 2 to 3 days in the fridge.*

CATEGORIES - *Economical · Entertaining · Lactose free · Vegetarian*

CONTINUED ON PAGE 238

CONTINUED FROM PAGE 236

238

INGREDIENTS

1 cup whole-wheat flour

1 ¼ cups all-purpose flour

4 large eggs, beaten

1 tbsp olive oil

½ tsp salt

STEPS

1   In a large bowl, combine the two types of flour. Make a well in the centre, and add the eggs, oil, and salt. Using your hands, gradually incorporate the flour until a dough forms. Form into a ball and knead for 5 minutes. Wrap the ball in plastic wrap, and set aside at room temperature for 30 minutes.

2   On a floured work surface, cut the ball of dough in half. Pass it through a pasta maker, according to the manufacturer's directions. You can also make pasta by hand, using a rolling pin to roll the dough out until very thin.

3   Cook immediately in a pot of salted boiling water for 1 to 3 minutes, depending on the thickness of the pasta.

1 — *You can complete the first step, and then refrigerate the ball of dough until needed. However, it'll be slightly more humid, so flour generously before rolling.*

2 — *A pasta maker can be mastered, and it's a lot of fun. It'll probably take a couple of tries before you get the hang of it. Be patient with yourself.*

3 — *If the pasta sticks, lightly flour it.*

4 — *If the pasta breaks while passing it through the pasta maker, fold it over itself and pass it a few times through the maker without reducing the thickness.*

5 — *Cooking homemade pasta is very quick and easy: boil for 1 to 3 minutes, depending on thickness. Ideally, the pasta should be tasted often to avoid overcooking.*

6 — *The pasta freezes well, as long as it's uncooked. To cook from frozen, simply put it (still frozen) into boiling water. The cooking time should be more or less the same.*

CHAPTER

No.⁸

—

VEGETABLES,
CASSEROLES & SIDES

HONEY MUSTARD–GLAZED CARROTS

HIS CHOICE

BEST BEFORE

Keeps for 3 to 4 days in the fridge.

CATEGORIES

Economical · Entertaining · Quick & easy · Lactose free · Gluten free · Vegetarian

VEGETABLES, CASSEROLES & SIDES

INGREDIENTS

3 cups peeled or scrubbed carrot sticks, rounds, or whole carrots

1 tbsp olive oil

1 clove garlic, chopped

Salt and pepper, to taste

¼ cup chopped fresh parsley

FOR THE SAUCE

2 tbsp honey

¼ cup apple juice

1 tbsp grainy mustard

STEPS

1   Bring a pot of water to a boil, and add the carrots. Boil for 2 to 5 minutes, depending on the size of carrots (5 minutes if big and whole, 2 minutes if cut into rounds). Drain, and rinse under very cold water. Drain again, and set aside.

2   In a bowl, combine all the sauce ingredients. Set aside.

3   In a pan, over high heat, heat the olive oil. Add the carrots and garlic, and sauté for 2 minutes. Add the sauce, season, and continue cooking for 3 minutes. Add the parsley, adjust the seasoning to taste, and serve.

TIP

If you like cumin, I recommend adding ½ teaspoon ground cumin to the sauce.

When I was young, I used to copy my cousins' or friends' tastes. If one of them hated mushrooms, I'd hate mushrooms. I probably did this so people would like me, and so I could be just like everyone else. And that's exactly what happened with Brussels sprouts, which I hated. I'd need the help of bacon to enjoy this herbaceous plant from the Brassica family (thanks, Wikipedia).

So, I'm pleased to share this recipe that's likely to convince even the staunchest skeptics, myself included, that Brussels sprouts are amazing.

HIS
CHOICE

BRUSSELS SPROUTS WITH BACON & ALMONDS

QUANTITY : *4 servings* · 🥄 5 MIN · 🕐 15 MIN · *Freezes well.*

BEST BEFORE — *Keeps for 3 to 4 days in the fridge.*

CATEGORIES — *Economical · Quick & easy · Lactose free · Gluten free*

INGREDIENTS

1 tbsp butter

4 strips bacon, finely chopped

3 cups Brussels sprouts, trimmed and halved

Salt and pepper, to taste

⅓ cup water

¼ cup toasted sliced almonds

1 tbsp balsamic vinegar

STEPS

1 In a pan, over medium-high heat, melt the butter. Add the bacon, and sauté for 2 minutes. Add the Brussels sprouts, and continue cooking for 7 to 8 minutes, stirring occasionally, until golden brown. Season.

2 Add the water, and continue cooking for about 4 minutes. Once the liquid has evaporated, add the almonds and balsamic vinegar. Stir well. Adjust the seasoning to taste, and serve.

SPAGHETTI SQUASH, BROCCOLI & SWISS CHEESE CASSEROLE

BEST BEFORE - *Keeps for 3 to 4 days in the fridge.*

CATEGORIES - *Indulgent · Entertaining · Vegetarian*

INGREDIENTS

1 medium spaghetti squash

¼ cup butter

¼ cup all-purpose flour

1 ½ cups milk

1 tbsp salted herbs

2 cups grated Swiss cheese

6 cups (1 package) baby spinach

1 head broccoli, cut into small florets

Salt and pepper, to taste

STEPS

1   Preheat the oven to 375°F, with the rack in centre position.

2   Halve the spaghetti squash and remove the seeds. Wrap each half in plastic wrap, and cook in the microwave on High for 8 minutes. Using a fork, shred the flesh, which should resemble spaghetti, and set aside.

3   In a large pot, over medium heat, melt the butter. Whisk in the flour to form a paste. Gradually add the milk, continually whisking to avoid lumps, and bring to a boil.

4   Stir in the salted herbs, and 1 cup of the cheese. Add the spaghetti squash, spinach, and broccoli. Season.

5   Transfer the mixture to a baking dish, and top with the remaining cheese.

6   Bake for 20 minutes. To finish, broil until nicely golden brown on top.

ORZO WITH ASPARAGUS, LEMON & PARMESAN

BEST BEFORE - *Keeps for 3 to 4 days in the fridge.*

CATEGORIES - *Economical · Quick & easy · Lactose free · Vegetarian*

INGREDIENTS

1 cup orzo

2 cups chopped asparagus

½ cup olive oil

2 whole cloves garlic, smashed

Juice of 1 lemon

½ cup freshly grated Parmesan cheese

Salt and pepper, to taste

STEPS

1 Bring a large pot of water to a boil. Cook the orzo according to the package directions. One minute before the end of the cook time, add the asparagus. Cook for 1 minute, then drain. Transfer to a bowl and set aside.

2 In a pan, over low heat, heat the olive oil and garlic for 5 minutes, so the garlic infuses the oil. Remove the garlic cloves from the pan, and pour the oil over the orzo and asparagus.

3 Add the remaining ingredients, stir well, and serve.

TIP

Serve this side dish at room temperature, cold, or hot.

PORTOBELLOS STUFFED WITH GOAT CHEESE

BEST BEFORE - *Keeps for 3 to 4 days in the fridge.*

CATEGORIES - *Entertaining · Vegetarian*

INGREDIENTS

2 tbsp olive oil

4 whole portobello mushrooms

FOR THE STUFFING

1 tbsp butter

2 shallots or green onions, finely sliced

2 cloves garlic, chopped

1 tbsp balsamic vinegar

¼ cup crumbled goat cheese

1 ½ cups cubed (½ inch) baguette bread

1 egg, beaten

½ tsp ground nutmeg

2 tbsp chopped fresh parsley

Salt and pepper, to taste

STEPS

1   Preheat the oven to 350°F, with the rack in centre position.

2   In a pan, over medium-high heat, melt the butter. Add the shallots and garlic, and sauté for 3 to 4 minutes. Deglaze the pan with the balsamic vinegar. Transfer to a bowl.

3   Add the goat cheese, and stir until melted. Add the remaining stuffing ingredients, and stir well. Set aside.

4   Remove the mushroom stems, oil the outsides of the mushrooms, and place gill side up on a baking sheet. Spoon some stuffing on top of each. Bake for 15 minutes. Serve.

TIP

This recipe goes really well with steak.

CHICKPEA, SQUASH & KALE STEW WITH LIME YOGURT

INGREDIENTS

1 tbsp olive oil

1 yellow onion, chopped

2 cloves garlic, chopped

2 tbsp chopped peeled fresh ginger

Salt and pepper, to taste

1 can (28 oz) diced tomatoes

1 can (19 oz) chickpeas, rinsed and drained

3 cups peeled and cubed butternut squash

1 cup chicken broth (or vegetable broth)

1 bunch kale, leaves only, finely sliced

FOR THE SPICE MIX

3 cardamom pods, ground

¼ tsp ground cloves

1 tsp ground turmeric

1 tsp ground coriander seeds

1 tsp ground cumin

1 tbsp brown sugar

FOR THE YOGURT

½ cup plain yogurt

Zest and juice of 1 lime

Salt and pepper, to taste

BEST BEFORE
Keeps for about 1 week in the fridge.

CATEGORIES
Economical · Gluten free · Vegetarian

STEPS

1   In a bowl, combine all the yogurt ingredients. Cover and refrigerate.

2   In another bowl, combine all the spice mix ingredients. Set aside.

3   In a pot, over medium heat, heat the olive oil. Add the onion, garlic, and ginger, and sauté for 3 minutes. Season, and stir in the spices. Continue cooking for 1 minute.

4   Add the tomatoes, chickpeas, squash, and broth. Season again, and bring to a boil. Reduce the heat to low and simmer for 15 minutes.

5   Add the kale, stir, cover the pot with the lid, and continue cooking for 8 minutes. Adjust the seasoning to taste. Serve with the yogurt.

HOMEMADE GREEK
POTATO POUTINE

QUANTITY : *4 servings* · 🍴 15 MIN · 🕐 30 MIN · *Freezes well.*

I never wanted to reinvent poutine. Tons of restaurants do it better than me and, honestly, I've never had a poutine that tops the classic version. I'm just not someone who's crazy about sausage, pulled pork, or spaghetti sauce on my poutine. Go ahead and judge!

Give me cheese, potatoes, good gravy, and more cheese. Simple as that! So that's what I'm offering, only with a cute twist on the potatoes, prepared Greek-style, and a little cream added to the gravy — nothing drastic, but it adds a little *je ne sais quoi*, making the whole dish a little more indulgent.

CONTINUED ON PAGE 256

CONTINUED FROM PAGE 254

BEST BEFORE - *Keeps for 2 to 3 days in the fridge.*

CATEGORIES - *Economical · Indulgent · Gluten free*

256

INGREDIENTS

1 bag cheese curds

FOR THE POTATOES

5 to 6 Yukon Gold potatoes, quartered

1 tbsp chopped fresh oregano

2 tsp onion powder

½ tsp salt

1 tsp sweet paprika

A small pinch (about ¼ tsp) Cayenne pepper (optional)

¼ cup vegetable oil

FOR THE GRAVY

2 tbsp cornstarch diluted in 3 tbsp water

1 ½ cups beef broth

1 tbsp ketchup

2 tsp Dijon mustard

¼ tsp garlic powder

½ tsp onion powder

1 tsp Worcestershire sauce

2 tbsp 35% cream

STEPS

FOR THE POTATOES

1   Preheat the oven to 425°F, with the rack in centre position. Line a baking sheet with parchment paper, and set aside.

2   In a large bowl, combine all the potato ingredients. Spread on the baking sheet, and bake for 15 minutes. Flip the potatoes, and continue baking for 15 minutes.

FOR THE GRAVY

3   In a small pot, combine all the sauce ingredients. Whisk, and bring to a boil. Simmer for 2 minutes.

ASSEMBLY

4   Roughly chop the cheese curds.

5   Put the potatoes on a plate, top with the cheese, and pour hot gravy over everything. Serve.

Whole, grilled cauliflower is all the rage, but it only comes out well on Pinterest, in my opinion. In reality, it's the type of recipe with a deceptive exterior, since the middle either doesn't taste like anything or is hard and raw. You know what I'm talking about.

I decided to come up with a really tasty version that would please everyone: by cutting the cauliflower into quarters. It's Pinterest that's practical — the best kind.

258

ROASTED CAULIFLOWER QUARTERS WITH CAPER & SUNDRIED TOMATO SAUCE

BEST BEFORE - *Keeps for 3 to 4 days in the fridge.*

CATEGORIES - *Economical · Lactose free · Gluten free · Vegetarian*

INGREDIENTS

1 head cauliflower

2 tbsp olive oil

1 tbsp butter

Salt and pepper, to taste

FOR THE SAUCE

2 tbsp melted butter

1 clove garlic, chopped

2 tbsp chopped fresh parsley

1 tsp sweet paprika

1 tbsp capers, drained and chopped

⅓ cup sundried tomatoes, chopped

2 tbsp sherry vinegar

½ cup chicken broth (or vegetable broth)

STEPS

1   In a bowl, combine all the sauce ingredients. Set aside.

2   Preheat the oven to 400°F, with the rack in centre position.

3   Trim the cauliflower stalk to remove the leaves, then cut the whole head of cauliflower into quarters. Set aside.

4   In a large pan, over high heat, heat the olive oil and butter. Sauté the cauliflower quarters for 3 to 4 minutes on each side, until golden brown.

5   Transfer the cauliflower to an oven-safe dish, season generously, and pour over all the sauce.

6   Bake for 15 minutes. Serve the cauliflower doused in the nice, hot sauce.

VEGETARIAN LASAGNA TART

BEST BEFORE - *Keeps for 2 to 3 days in the fridge.*

CATEGORIES - *Indulgent · Vegetarian*

INGREDIENTS

1 store-bought or homemade pastry tart shell or dough

2 tbsp plain breadcrumbs

1 ½ cups shredded mozzarella cheese

FOR THE VEGETABLE MIXTURE

1 tbsp olive oil

1 zucchini, cut into rounds

1 package (8 oz) white button mushrooms, finely sliced

1 clove garlic, chopped

Salt and pepper, to taste

1 cup store-bought tomato sauce

6 cups baby spinach

¼ cup sundried tomatoes, chopped

1 tbsp chopped fresh oregano

FOR THE RICOTTA

1 cup ricotta cheese

1 egg

Salt and pepper, to taste

STEPS

1 Preheat the oven to 375°F, with the rack in centre position.

2 Roll out the dough so it is big enough to line a 9-inch tart pan or pie dish. Dust the bottom of the pie shell with the breadcrumbs. Set aside.

3 In a pan, over high heat, heat the olive oil. Add the zucchini rounds, mushrooms, and garlic, and sauté for 5 minutes. Season.

4 Stir in the remaining vegetable mixture ingredients, reduce the heat to low, and cook for 8 minutes. Adjust the seasoning to taste, and set aside.

5 In a bowl, whisk together all the ricotta ingredients, and set aside.

6 Spread half of the vegetable mixture over the pastry. Top with the ricotta mixture, and then the rest of the vegetables. Sprinkle all over with the mozzarella. Bake for 40 minutes.

VEGETABLES, CASSEROLES & SIDES

GREEN BEANS WITH COCONUT "BREADCRUMBS"

BEST BEFORE - *Keeps for 3 to 4 days in the fridge.*

CATEGORIES - *Economical · Quick & easy · Lactose free · Gluten free · Vegetarian*

INGREDIENTS

2 cups green or yellow beans, trimmed

1 tbsp olive oil

Salt and pepper, to taste

Juice of 1 lime

2 tbsp soy sauce (or tamari)

2 tbsp chopped fresh cilantro

3 tbsp fine unsweetened shredded coconut

STEPS

1   Bring a large pot of water to a boil. Add the beans, and cook for 2 minutes. Drain in a colander, and rinse under cold water to stop the cooking.

2   In a large pan, over medium heat, heat the olive oil. Add the beans, and sauté for 1 minute. Season.

3   Stir in the remaining ingredients, and continue cooking for 2 minutes. Adjust the seasoning to taste, and serve.

I made this tart using raw beets because it saves a lot of time and keeps the beets slightly crunchy, which I love! However, if you have leftover cooked beets, they'll work just as well; simply cut them into slices as thin as you like.

THIN CRUST BEET & CHEESE TART

265

BEST BEFORE - *Keeps for 3 to 4 days in the fridge.*

CATEGORIES - *Entertaining · Vegetarian*

INGREDIENTS

3 cups sliced peeled raw or cooked beets (see headnote; cut into very thin slices)

2 tbsp olive oil

1 clove garlic, chopped

Salt and pepper, to taste

1 package (14 oz) store-bought puff pastry

2 tbsp Dijon mustard

FOR THE TOPPING

¼ cup chopped fresh parsley

½ cup crumbled cheese of your choice (blue, feta, or goat)

Zest of 1 lemon (or more, to taste)

⅓ cup pecans, chopped

STEPS

1   Preheat the oven to 350°F, with the rack in centre position. Line a baking sheet with parchment paper. Set aside.

2   In a bowl, combine the beets, olive oil, and garlic. Season generously, and set aside.

3   On a floured work surface, roll out the puff pastry to form a 14-inch × 10-inch rectangle. Transfer to the baking sheet, and slather the pastry surface with Dijon mustard. Arrange the beets on the pastry, and bake for 45 minutes.

4   In a bowl, combine all the topping ingredients. Spread over the beets. Return to the oven and bake for 5 minutes. Serve.

CHAPTER

No.⁹

—

DESSERTS

○
HIS
CHOICE

QUANTITY : *8 servings* · 🥄 40 MIN · 🕐 45 MIN · ☾ 2 H · *Freezes well.*

CARROT, APPLE & MAPLE CAKE

BEST BEFORE - *Keeps for 4 to 5 days in the fridge.*

CATEGORIES - *Indulgent · Entertaining · Vegetarian*

I know a lot of people who add pineapple to their carrot cake, and I admit the result is pretty delicious, but wait until you try my version with grated apples and applesauce. The taste is subtly different, and I'd venture to add that both ingredients add favourably to the cake's texture, making it really moist. This recipe has quickly become a Champagne family classic.

CONTINUED ON PAGE 270

CONTINUED FROM PAGE 269

INGREDIENTS

DRY INGREDIENTS

2 cups all-purpose flour

½ tsp baking soda

1 tsp baking powder

A pinch of salt

WET INGREDIENTS

3 large eggs, lightly beaten

1 cup unsweetened applesauce, homemade or store-bought

½ cup vegetable oil

1 cup sugar

½ cup maple syrup

2 cups peeled and grated carrots

1 cup peeled, cored, and grated apples

1 tsp ground cinnamon

½ tsp ground allspice

1 tsp vanilla extract

FOR THE TOPPING

½ cup chopped walnuts

1 tbsp maple syrup

FOR THE ICING

9 oz cream cheese, at room temperature

½ cup maple syrup

4 ¼ cups icing sugar

1   Preheat the oven to 350°F, with the rack in centre position. Grease and flour two 9-inch cake pans, and set aside.

2   In a bowl, combine all the dry ingredients. Set aside.

3   In another bowl, stir together all the wet ingredients. Add the dry ingredients, and stir well. Divide the mixture evenly between the two pans, and bake for 45 minutes, or until a toothpick inserted in the centre comes out clean. Let cool completely in pans at room temperature.

4   Line a baking sheet with parchment paper, and set aside.

5   In a bowl, combine the walnuts and maple syrup. Spread over the baking sheet. Bake for 12 minutes. Let cool.

6   In a large bowl, using an electric mixer, beat together the cream cheese and maple syrup. While continuing to mix, gradually incorporate the icing sugar until the mixture reaches a nice consistency. Set aside.

7   Using a serrated knife, cut a bit off the top of one of the cakes, so it's flat, and place it cut side down on a serving plate. Spread with icing. Place the second cake on top, then cover the entire cake with the remaining icing. Top with maple walnuts. Serve.

The idea for this recipe came to me after eating a fruit salad while sipping a cup of really hot tea. The difference in temperatures meant that every time I bit into a piece of fruit, I'd get brain freeze, and I hated that sensation. However, because the flavours were so good together, I decided to combine them into one delicious recipe, for the benefit of my taste buds and my teeth. Yay!

While we're on the subject, I much prefer to eat fruit that's at room temperature. I've never understood how people can gobble up a plate of cold strawberries when they're so much better and juicier at room temperature. Same goes for tomatoes. Try it — you'll taste the difference.

BEST BEFORE   -   *Keeps for 3 to 4 days in the fridge.*

CATEGORIES   -   *Entertaining · Quick & easy · Lactose free · Gluten free · Vegetarian*

INGREDIENTS

FOR THE TEA

¼ cup honey (or maple syrup)

½ cup water

Seeds from 1 vanilla bean (see tip below)

1 Earl Grey tea bag

FOR THE FRUIT SALAD

6 plums, pitted and cut into chunks

2 cups seedless red grapes, halved

2 cups strawberries, quartered

1 cup blackberries

3 cups cubed (½ inch) cantaloupe

8 to 10 fresh mint leaves, chopped

STEPS

1   In a small pot, combine the honey, water, and vanilla. Bring to a boil. Remove the pan from the heat and add the tea bag. Steep for 2 minutes, then discard the tea bag. Refrigerate for 15 minutes.

2   Place all the fruit in a bowl, and add the tea syrup. Stir well, and let marinate for a minimum of 20 minutes before serving.

TIP

Vanilla beans are readily available at grocery stores, often in the same place you find sugar, vanilla, and flour. To remove the seeds, simply cut the bean lengthwise in two and scrape out the middle using a knife.

FRUIT SALAD WITH TEA

QUANTITY : *8–10 servings* · 🥄 25 MIN · 🕐 3 MIN · 🌙 35 MIN · *Doesn't freeze well.*

DOUBLE CHOCOLATE & MAPLE POOR MAN'S PUDDING

BEST BEFORE - *Keeps for 4 to 5 days in the fridge.*

CATEGORIES - *Indulgent · Entertaining · Vegetarian*

INGREDIENTS

1 ½ cups all-purpose flour

2 tsp baking powder

A pinch of salt

1 cup sugar

½ cup butter, at room temperature

1 egg

1 cup milk

3 ½ oz dark (70%) chocolate, roughly chopped

3 ½ oz white chocolate, roughly chopped

FOR THE SAUCE

1 cup maple syrup

1 cup brown sugar

1 cup 35% cream

STEPS

1   Preheat the oven to 350°F, with the rack in centre position. Grease a 13-inch × 9-inch baking pan. Set aside.

2   In a pot, combine all the sauce ingredients, and bring to a boil. Remove the pan from the heat, and set aside.

3   In a bowl, combine the flour, baking powder, and salt. Set aside.

4   In another bowl, whisk together the sugar and butter until creamy. Add the egg, and whisk well.

5   In alternating batches, stir in the flour mixture and milk. Add the chocolate, gently stir, and pour into the baking pan.

6   Pour the sauce over the dough (do not stir), and bake for about 35 minutes, or until the top is slightly golden.

CREAM CHEESE, LIME, KIWI & ALMOND CRUMBLE DESSERT SHOOTERS

276

BEST BEFORE - *Keeps for 2 to 3 days in the fridge.*

CATEGORIES - *Economical · Entertaining · Quick & easy · Vegetarian*

INGREDIENTS

4 kiwis, peeled and quartered

FOR THE CRUMBLE

2 tbsp whole-wheat flour

¼ cup oatmeal

¼ cup slivered almonds

2 tbsp butter, melted

2 tbsp honey

FOR THE CHEESE

½ cup cream cheese

½ cup plain Greek yogurt

3 tbsp honey

Zest of 1 lime

Juice of ½ lime

STEPS

1   Preheat the oven to 350°F, with the rack in centre position. Line a baking sheet with parchment paper. Set aside.

2   In a bowl, combine all the crumble ingredients. Spread over the baking sheet. Bake for 15 minutes. Let cool for 5 minutes, then loosely crumble. Set aside.

3   In another bowl, whisk together all the cheese ingredients. Set aside.

4   In four dessert glasses, layer kiwi, cheese, crumble, and kiwi again to finish. Serve.

TIP

This dessert is ideal for entertaining because it keeps for up to 3 days in the fridge. However, for best results I recommend assembling it at the last minute.

VANILLA CRÈME
BRÛLÉE

RECIPE ON PAGE 280

280

VANILLA CRÈME BRÛLÉE

PHOTO ON PAGE 278

This recipe comes courtesy of our friend Gustav, who makes the best crème
brûlées in the world. He agreed to reveal his secrets and share this recipe with
us for the book, which makes me really happy.

QUANTITY : *6 servings* · 🥄 15 MIN · 🕐 35 MIN · ☾ 2 H · *Doesn't freeze well.*

BEST BEFORE - *Keeps for 4 to 5 days in the fridge.*

CATEGORIES - *Economical · Indulgent · Gluten free · Vegetarian*

INGREDIENTS

8 egg yolks

½ cup sugar

2 cups 35% cream

Seeds from 1 vanilla bean (see tip on page 272)

4 tbsp sugar (for the caramelized crust)

STEPS

1   Preheat the oven to 350°F, with the rack in centre position.

2   In a bowl, using an electric mixer, beat together the egg yolks and sugar for 5 minutes, or until light and creamy. While mixing, gradually add the cream and vanilla.

3   Place six ½-cup ramekins in an oven-safe dish. Divide the mixture among them.

4   Carefully, pour water into the oven-safe dish until it reaches halfway up the sides of the ramekins, making sure the water doesn't spill into the ramekins or the cream won't set.

5   Bake for 35 minutes.

6   Let cool, and then refrigerate the ramekins for a minimum of 2 hours.

7   Dust the surface of each brûlée with a thin layer of sugar. Using a kitchen torch, caramelize the sugar. If you don't have a kitchen torch, place the ramekins on a baking sheet, adjust the oven rack to the highest position, and broil them until the sugar caramelizes.

TIP

I recommend saving the egg whites to make a nice, healthy omelette the next morning.

HIS
CHOICE

BLUEBERRY & BANANA CLAFOUTIS

283

BEST BEFORE - *Keeps for 3 to 4 days in the fridge.*

CATEGORIES - *Entertaining · Quick & easy · Vegetarian*

INGREDIENTS

1 ripe banana

½ cup sugar

3 eggs

¾ cup plain yogurt (or vanilla)

1 tsp vanilla extract

½ cup 35% cream

2 tbsp butter, melted

1 cup all-purpose flour

A pinch of salt

2 cups (1 heaping pint) blueberries

Whipped cream, for serving

STEPS

1 Preheat the oven to 350°F, with the rack in centre position. Grease a 10-inch pie plate and set aside.

2 In a bowl, mash the banana with a fork. Add the sugar, eggs, yogurt, and vanilla, and whisk well. Add the cream and butter.

3 Add the flour and salt, and whisk into a smooth batter. Transfer the mixture to the pie plate.

4 Lightly press the blueberries into the top of the batter.

5 Bake for 40 minutes. Let cool before serving with whipped cream.

The beauty of an old-fashioned tart is that you don't have to worry about getting the crust perfect. In fact, it's often better when it's a little broken and flawed. When I'm feeling particularly adventurous, I sprinkle a few chocolate chips into my fruit mixture and I'm never disappointed. Enjoy!

BEST BEFORE - *Keeps for 3 to 4 days in the fridge.*

CATEGORIES - *Economical · Entertaining · Vegetarian*

INGREDIENTS

OLD-FASHIONED TART CRUST

1 ¼ cups whole-wheat flour

½ cup cold butter, cut into small cubes

¼ cup sugar

1 egg

FOR THE FILLING

½ cup ricotta cheese

¼ cup brown sugar

2 cups berries (see tip below)

2 tbsp butter, melted

STEPS

1 In a bowl, combine the flour and butter. Using your hands, work the butter into the flour until the texture resembles coarse sand. Add the sugar and egg, and stir just until a dough forms. Knead lightly to form a ball. Divide the dough into four equal portions, and wrap each in plastic wrap. Refrigerate for 30 minutes. Set aside.

2 Preheat the oven to 350°F, with the rack in centre position. Line a baking sheet with parchment paper. Set aside.

3 In a bowl, combine the ricotta and brown sugar. Set aside.

4 On a floured work surface, roll each ball of dough into a circle about 15 cm in diameter.

5 Transfer the crusts to the baking sheet, and spread each with 3 tbsp of the cheese mixture. Top with the fruit. Gently fold the sides up over the topping.

6 Brush the fruit-filled crusts with melted butter. Bake for 30 minutes.

7 Dust with icing sugar or serve with ice cream.

DESSERTS

TIP

Feel free to mix lots of different fruits together: raspberries, blackberries, strawberries, blueberries, cherries, etc. If you're using bigger fruits, just make sure to cut them into small pieces.

OLD-FASHIONED RICOTTA
& BERRY TARTLETS

PEAR & DATE CAKE
WITH AMARETTO

QUANTITY : *8 servings* · 🥄 15 MIN · 🕐 1 H 15 · 🌙 1 H · *Freezes well.*

The night I was supposed to prepare this recipe so we could photograph it the next day, I was too tired from too many sleepless nights. Alex decided to pick up the slack and let me sleep, following every step of this recipe to the letter.

When I awoke early the next morning, the smell of cake filled the house and the kitchen was a mess. I had to admit that it tasted really good, and I smiled to myself in the knowledge that even first-time cooks could turn this recipe into a masterpiece.

BEST BEFORE - *Keeps for 4 to 5 days in the fridge.*

CATEGORIES - *Gift · Entertaining · Lactose free · Vegetarian*

INGREDIENTS

1 dozen large Medjool dates, pitted and halved

½ cup almond liqueur (Amaretto)

1 ¾ cups all-purpose flour

1 tsp baking soda

A pinch of salt

2 eggs, beaten

¾ cup coconut sugar (or regular sugar)

¾ cup vegetable oil

¼ cup maple syrup

1 cup peeled, cored, and grated Bosc pears (about 1 pear)

STEPS

1 In a bowl, combine the dates and Amaretto. Let marinate for a minimum of 1 hour or overnight. Set aside.

2 Preheat the oven to 350°F, with the rack in centre position. Grease a loaf pan, and set aside.

3 In a bowl, combine the flour, baking soda, and salt. Set aside.

4 In another bowl, whisk together the eggs and sugar. Stir in the oil, maple syrup, and pear. Add the flour mixture, and stir well. Set aside.

5 Using a fork, roughly mash the dates in the Amaretto, so they break up a bit. Add to the flour mixture (including any Amaretto remaining in the bowl). Stir well. Pour the batter into the bread pan. Bake for 1 hour, or until a toothpick inserted in the centre comes out clean.

6 Let cool before serving.

You can serve this dessert in normal-size bowls, if you wish, but it's fun to serve it in hollowed-out lemons. Sorbet is easy to make ahead, and can be served right out of the freezer. Guests will really like it, too. It's something that my mom sometimes buys at a little store near her place and that I've always wanted to make at home.

BEST BEFORE

Keeps for a few weeks in the freezer in a sealed container.

CATEGORIES

Entertaining · Quick & easy · Gluten free · Vegetarian

INGREDIENTS

7 lemons

¾ cup mascarpone cheese

½ cup sugar

⅓ cup honey

½ cup water

4 sprigs thyme,
leaves only, chopped (optional)

STEPS

1   Cut the lemons in half, and squeeze 1 cup of juice. Set the juice aside.

2   Using a spoon, scoop out the lemon flesh from each lemon and discard. Using a knife, cut the bottom of each flat, so they stand up. Set aside.

3   In a bowl, whisk together the mascarpone and sugar. Add the reserved lemon juice, and the honey, water, and thyme. Stir well, and transfer to a sealed container. Freeze for a minimum of 8 hours. After about 3 hours, stir the mixture once and return to the freezer.

4   Fill the lemon halves with sorbet, and store in a sealed container in the freezer. Serve when ready.

MASCARPONE, LEMON & HONEY SORBET

QUANTITY : *8 servings* · 🥄 15 MIN · ☾ 8 H · *Freezes well*

CASHEW CHOCOLATE
MOUSSE

290

BEST BEFORE - *Keeps for 1 week in the fridge.*

CATEGORIES - *Indulgent · Entertaining · Gluten free · Vegetarian*

INGREDIENTS

2 cups unsalted raw cashews

¼ cup cocao powder

¼ cup maple syrup (or agave or honey)

2 tbsp coconut oil

⅓ cup brewed espresso (see tip below)

⅓ cup 35% cream

FOR THE TOPPING

Malted milk balls

Slivered almonds, toasted (or other nuts)

Chocolate shavings

Fresh berries

STEPS

1   Place the cashews in a small bowl and cover with water. Let soak overnight or for a minimum of 2 hours. Drain.

2   In a food processor, combine all the ingredients, with the exception of the cream, and process for 5 minutes, or until smooth and creamy. Set aside.

3   Whip the cream, and gently fold it into the mixture. Divide mousse between four jars, and refrigerate for a minimum of 30 minutes. Serve with the topping of your choice.

TIP

I consider the coffee in this dessert a must, but you can replace it with vanilla almond milk, if you prefer. Alternatively, if you like the taste of coffee but not its effect, feel free to use decaf.

GIANT CHOCOLATE CHIP & MARSHMALLOW COOKIE CASSEROLE

HIS CHOICE

BEST BEFORE

Keeps in a sealed container for 2 to 3 days at room temperature.

CATEGORIES

Economical · Indulgent · Entertaining · Quick & easy · Lactose free · Vegetarian

INGREDIENTS

1 cup all-purpose flour

1 tsp baking powder

½ tsp salt

¾ cup brown sugar

½ cup butter, softened

1 egg

½ cup dark chocolate chips

¾ cup mini marshmallows

Ice cream, or sorbet, for serving

STEPS

1   Preheat the oven to 350°F, with the rack in centre position. Grease a 9-inch casserole dish, pie dish, or oven-safe dish. Set aside.

2   In a bowl, combine the flour, baking powder, and salt. Set aside.

3   Using an electric mixer, beat together the brown sugar and butter. Add the egg, and beat until smooth.

4   Add the flour mixture, and stir well. Fold in the chocolate chips and marshmallows.

5   Spread the dough evenly in the pan. Bake for 18 minutes. Serve immediately with ice cream.

DESSERTS

TIP

You can prepare the cookie dough in advance and store it in the fridge. Simply let it warm up for 15 to 20 minutes at room temperature before baking.

ACKNOWLEDGEMENTS

MARILOU

—

This book is not just a collection of recipes; it's the product of much love, talent, giving, energy, humour, imagination, depth, and the many other strengths (and some imperfections) of the wonderful team around me, who help me grow every day. This is a team of extremely respectful and honest people, who I've had the huge privilege of being able to assemble from my heart and without whom I definitely wouldn't have had the courage to try to improve people's relationship with food. They mirror my creativity and, without knowing it, they help me to learn and flourish. I want to thank them.

Alex, my husband, thank you for giving us permission to not be perfect and even to appreciate our imperfections. As a result, the most difficult days have become my favourite, because that's when we talk and understand each other better and I feel like I'm taking a huge step towards you, which brings us closer. And my favourite place in the world is right next to you. When I look at our book, that's what I see: the culmination of all our work and the journey our two souls took to get here, getting lost and found as we weathered life's little challenges, which sometimes got the better of us, but never enough to drive us apart. I love you.

Véronique Paradis, every time you look at a recipe and exclaim "that's niiiiiice" in an old man's voice, I'm over the moon. You're probably the most reliable, efficient, and persevering person I know, on top of being honest, diplomatic, and direct. You work hard, without fanfare, and are always in a good mood, which pretty much guarantees a positive atmosphere for everyone around you. Thank you. And a little "hello" to Loulou.

Andréane Beaudin, you see the good in everything, which not only brightens our work, but my whole day.

Anne Sylvestre, thank you for not being married to your ideas. You lay your talent on the table, like a gift, selflessly, and offer us the best parts, which is truly inspiring. It's rare for a gifted artist's humility to be proportional to her talent.

Dad, thank you for coming to wash the dishes on the days we were photographing the book's recipes. Your "Bonne Maman" apron and jokes did me a world of good.

Mom and Natasha, little Jeanne's official babysitters, without whom we never would have been able to focus on the book's photos. Seeing you laughing with Jeanne and loving her, right next to me as I was working, was comforting beyond words. Thank you.

Mélanie Dubé, thank you for taking the words right out of my mouth, and often making them better than they were in my head.

To the entire team at Trois fois par jour, as well as Geneviève Rivard, a member of the extended family: words cannot describe how lucky I am to have you in my life.

To Antoine Ross Trempe, whose initials make me insanely jealous, and the entire team at Éditions Cardinal: thank you for encouraging me. You're there when things aren't going well, when everything's all right, and the rest of the time in between, no matter what the circumstances, which is very reassuring. Thank you.

To my readers, who I communicate with daily: thank you for accepting me as I am, for speaking to me as a friend, for confiding in me via private messages, for trusting me, for laughing with me, and for respecting my choices. Thank you for inspiring me, and in turn, being inspired by my work.

And finally, thank you to my sweet Jeanne, because, from now on, there'll always be a little bit of you in everything I do. I love you.

ALEX

—

Marilou, my wife, my colleague, my soulmate. For your patience, your kindness, and your willingness to do things in the truest way possible, without compromising our values. I love you.

Jeanne, my little treasure, because I forget all my problems when you smile at me while we're getting up.

Gus, Sofia, Anne, Véro, and Andrew, the dream team, the Harlem Globetrotters of the small business world, without the jerseys and the big, loose shorts.

Simon-Pierre Gingras, for having the wisdom to point me towards photography, after I graduated from The National Comedy School, and for your talent that continues to inspire me to this day.

Youri Bourdon, for being yourself.

Mom and Dad, for obvious reasons.

Antoine Ross Trempe, our beloved editor and business partner. An incredible visionary and an all-around great guy. I've got nothing but good things to say about you.

All of you, who bought our first book and this one. You're the reason our project is alive and well. Thank you from the bottom of my heart.

INDEX

In alphabetical order

INDEX

By chapter

309

INDEX

By category

ENTERTAINING

QUICK & EASY

INDEX BY CATEGORY

312

VEGETARIAN